CREATIVE
HOMEOWNER®

DESIGN IDEAS FOR
basements

CREATIVE HOMEOWNER®, Upper Saddle River, New Jersey

VP, Editorial Director: Timothy O. Bakke
Production Manager: Kimberly H. Vivas

Senior Editor: Kathie Robitz
Photo Editor/Researcher: Jennifer Ramcke
Editorial Assistant: Jennifer Doolittle

Senior Designer: Glee Barre
Cover Photography: Phillip Ennis
Cover Design: Glee Barre
Back Cover Photography: (clockwise) courtesy of Finnleo; Phillip Ennis; Phillip Ennis; courtesy of Whirlpool

Current Printing (last digit)
10 9 8 7 6 5 4 3 2 1

Manufactured in the United States of America

Design Ideas for Basements
Library of Congress Control Number: 2003112822
ISBN: 1-58011-158-0

CREATIVE HOMEOWNER®
A Division of Federal Marketing Corp.
24 Park Way
Upper Saddle River, NJ 07458
www.creativehomeowner.com

ACKNOWLEDGMENTS

To my loving family — Terri, Scott, Holly and Kelly — who were generous enough
to put up with my creative tension while writing this book. — W.K.

To my clients for letting me photograph their subjects; Carolyn Hecht for her research and
knowledge; and my loyal assistants who haul and rig the lights. — P.E.

contents

6

Transforming your basement into beautiful living space can increase the value of your home and enrich your life. What's more, the job is easier and less expensive than you might think.

The next 140 pages or so will provide you with a handsome portfolio of possibilities for redesigning your basement or redecorating one that is in drastic need of updating. No matter what your style or budget, you will find fresh ideas here that will challenge your notions of basement function and aesthetics.

The opening chapter underscores the benefits and convenience of adding room without adding on. Chapter 2 explains how to hide those ugly basement fixtures of furnace, oil tank, and water and gas pipes or, believe it or not, how to include them in your new design. It also offers practical solutions for eliminating moisture and mold and adding ventilation and soundproofing.

Looking for enlightening strategies to increase light and openness to a boxy, naturally dark basement? Chapter 3 offers the latest options in windows, and

you'll also get up to speed on basement doors—interior and exterior—that combine aesthetics and security.

You'll need to complement natural light with a range of artificial lighting strategies. Chapter 4 provides you with a full menu of solutions to brighten your new space and enhance its look.

Think of Chapters 5 through 10 as designer showrooms. They highlight the latest trends, materials, products, and design approaches for virtually any kind of room you might be thinking of creating: a media center, home office, family room (or the new "family studio"), kitchen, bedroom, bath, gym, spa, workshop, or laundry.

Design Ideas for Basements is all you need to come up with inspiration and know-how to meet your family's ever-changing and ever-growing needs for more space and greater comfort. After reading it you'll never look at your basement the same way again. Be sure to check the Resource Guide for information about manufacturers and professional associations that can also help you with your project.

OPPOSITE A home theater can make family movie night an especially entertaining experience.

LEFT Soft furnishings and rich colors add up to a cozy, comfortable setting for quiet time alone.

ABOVE A new bathroom with all of the trimmings increases the value of a house.

chapter one

adding

room

D o you need more living area? Do your domestic dreams
include a home office, a deluxe media room, or perhaps
a downstairs hangout for wild and crazy teens? Look no
further than under your feet. That's right, your humble
basement. In most cases, even the most ambitious project costs only a fraction of what you would spend to
build an addition. Estimates for building aboveground
average about $150 a foot; remodeling
a basement, on the other hand, usually
costs only $75 per foot—that's a 50-
percent savings.

LEFT A basement
space can be
fun, decorative,
and reflective
of all of your
interests.

The lower cost shouldn't surprise you. After all, a basement is fully enclosed and already comes with walls, a floor, and a ceiling. There's no need to spend major dollars breaking ground for an addition or to move to a new house in order to have that special hobby room or that extra bedroom.

What's more, no matter how grand your plan, remodeling your basement provides a major head start over new construction when it comes to heating and cooling the new space, powering a media room or home office, or meeting the additional plumbing needs of a bathroom or kitchen. The utilities are accessible and can be easily upgraded or adapted to accommodate your design needs.

Heating and cooling are usually a breeze. Basements are naturally cool in summer so air conditioning is often not required. Basements retain some of the residual heat from the furnace that warms up the main and upstairs living space. In colder areas, adding a few panels of baseboard heating can fill in the chilly gaps.

BELOW Don't settle for a plain living space. Enliven the room with glamour and flavor that will make it unforgettable to guests. Decorate it with an over-the-top theme or exotic accessories.

OPPOSITE Adding details to the room, such as an arched median and decorative wallcoverings, will leave family and friends wondering whether they are really in a basement.

BASIC BASEMENT TYPES

The type of basement you have may set up different challenges to overcome in your design, whether it is finishing surfaces, providing sources of ventilation, or choosing windows and doors that may be required by the new International Residential Code (IRC).

A standard basement is surrounded by belowground walls, with maybe 20 percent of the walls above grade. There might be small windows at the very top or none at all. You can access or exit this basement only through an interior stairway. There is very little light and limited air circulation. A concern may be the coolness of all that concrete, especially in winter.

A walk-out basement has at least one wall that is above grade. This allows more light into the interior. With windows and doors, a walk-out basement has more air circulation than a standard basement. Also, interior and exterior stairs provide greater access into and out of the basement, which makes this space highly usable for bedrooms.

upstairs,
downstairs

As increasing numbers of people spend more time at home, experts agree that they see their living space in a new way. People have come to realize that their homes are designable real estate that can meet changing needs and passions, rather than static rooms with rigid roles. And basements are, in many ways, the perfect space for that kind of flexible thinking and designing. The very shape of a basement—a long, shoebox-like room running the length of the house—is equivalent to a blank slate, beckoning you to leave your design imprint on it, whether your are creating a large space for the entire family or a suite of medium-sized rooms that serve an array of practical purposes.

In fact, the amorphous quality of a basement actually cries out for creativity and the kind of architectural interest and dimension that can transform it from unappealing to inviting. Think beyond knotty pine paneling and bean-bag chairs, and envision something more sophisticated. You can easily upgrade and enliven a boxy basement, for instance, by varying the height and angle of wall and ceiling planes. Mix materials, textures, and finishes on walls and ceilings. Include a greenhouse bumpout to bring the light and the outdoors into the space.

Let's assume your basement is dry and mold-free (See Chapter 2, "Taking Care of Basement Business," beginning on page 18, for tips on how to achieve both of those goals.) The choice of furniture, accessories, and window treatments can be limitless, and often no different from those you would use in the rest of the house.

OPPOSITE TOP A grand staiway can be a preview of the lush amenities downstairs.

OPPOSITE BOTTOM Set the mood with a surround-sound system built into the wall.

BELOW A theater-sized screen allows you to watch your favorite movie in plush style.

DREAM ON: FUTURE USES OF NEW SPACE

People and families change and, along with them, the rooms they inhabit. Before you commit to your basement's final design, make sure that you think through what you might need when the kids move out, you retire, or (gulp) your mother-in-law comes to live with you. The space you use for a playroom now may be converted into a guest suite or a home workshop in the future. Save time and money later by making sure the necessary wiring, plumbing, and mechanical work is roughed in before you cover the walls.

In order to imagine all of the possibilities, do some blue-sky thinking about 5 or 10 years down the line and create a checklist of possible needs for future configurations of your basement space.

RIGHT Stone, ironwork, and rough-hewn beams create an the Old World look in this setting.

BELOW Dinner is set in this romantic, softly lit wine cellar that was created in a remodeled basement.

ROOMS OF OPPORTUNITY

While some designers espouse tying the basement design into the home's overall style, others view basement conversions as a license to be daring. If you've always wanted to try a different look, go for it in the basement. Down-under spaces aren't seen from other levels, so there's no reason to take your design cues from upstairs. Here are some possibilities.

FAMILY ROOM This all-purpose living space is probably the easiest and least expensive way to add square footage to your home. You usually won't have to fiddle with or upgrade plumbing or worry about special egress windows. The main concern is keeping the space dry and selecting finishes for walls, floors, and ceilings that suit your taste and vision. Whether you are looking for space for the kids' toys and games or just a place where you can watch television, listen to music, or dance away the night, a family room is an ideal choice.

HOME OFFICE If you telecommute and need privacy and quiet to get your work done, designing a home office in the out-of-the-way basement is a no-brainer. Just make sure to include enough electrical circuits to power all of your equipment as well as any add-on technology in the future.

WINE CELLAR You might have always wanted one to house your collection of, say, Merlots or Syrahs, but couldn't find the right spot in your main living space. A cool, dark basement provides a perfect climate for your vintage hobby.

DESIGN TIP

Keep moldings simple in a basement with lower ceilings. Elaborate moldings around the ceiling or floor can shorten the height of the room.

BELOW It is essential to have plenty of storage space in a creative work area with a lot of implements.

CRAFTS STUDIO OR HOME WORKSHOP Perhaps you have a desire to take up landscape painting, to do some major crafting, or to try woodworking, but don't want to mess up the upstairs rooms or fill the house with paint fumes and dust. A downstairs arts-and-craft studio or home workshop, equipped with a quiet but powerful exhaust fan and a wall of storage bins can solve both problems and provide the privacy to enable you to complete your masterpiece. You might even combine this space with a laundry room, a trend that's called a "home studio." (See Chapter 6, beginning on page 76.)

MEDIA ROOM You don't need a fortune to create a highly entertaining media room for family and friends. It's easy to darken an already dim basement and to increase sound absorption with the right floor, wall, and ceiling materials. If you are ambitious, include a snack bar or kitchenette, complete with a refrigerator, sink, and microwave oven, so that you don't have to miss a moment of the movie.

SPA OR GYM After a long day's journey back from work, wouldn't it be relaxing to soak in a hot tub or melt away the tension in a sauna? Or reinvigorate yourself with a spin on the treadmill or elliptical trainer? Look to your basement, again. The concrete-slab floor requires no additional structural reinforcement to handle the substantial weight of a hot tub, which can weigh more than 4,000 pounds when filled to capacity, or heavy gym machines. Saunas—which usually come as prefabricated packages, complete with walls, floor, and ceiling—are the perfect amentiy for a windowless corner of the basement, and can often be tied into existing household circuits.

BEDROOM A basement is perfect for an extra bedroom. It typically has a bare minimum of natural light, and it's cool and quiet—a recipe for a good night's sleep.

EXTRA BATHROOM OR KITCHEN Adding an extra bathroom to a basement can free up space and thin out traffic upstairs and, when it's located near water-supply lines and a drain system, is easy and inexpensive to build. For the exact same reasons, adding a small kitchen won't break the bank.

ABOVE Workout time flies by while watching your favorite TV show or video.

OPPOSITE An extra bathroom in the basement can be glamorous.

RIGHT A basement bedroom is the ideal getaway from the upstairs traffic.

SIZING UP ROOMS

While there is no perfect-sized room—it depends on your needs and the space you have to work with—the U.S. Department of Housing and Urban Development (HUD) has come up with some recommendations, which are listed below. The minimum net floor area refers to the space within the enclosed walls and excludes built-in features such as cabinets and closets.

	MINIMUM AREA	MINIMUM SIZE	PREFERRED
Master Bedroom	n/a	n/a	2 x 16 ft.
Bedroom	80 sq. ft.	8 x 10 ft.	11 x 14 ft.
Family Room	110 sq. ft.	10.5 x 10.5 ft.	12 x 16 ft.
Living Room	176 sq. ft.	1 x 16 ft.	12 x 18 ft.
Great Room	n/a	n/a	14 x 20 ft.
Bathroom	35 sq. ft.	5 x 7 ft.	5 x 9 ft.

basement business

I

t takes real imagination to see beyond the dingy, grimy, and often ugly fixtures of a basement to a bright and airy living space where you will actually want to listen to music or entertain friends. Inevitable questions pop up: What can you do with that oversized oil tank? How can you hide those overhead gas and water pipes? And what about those metal poles that dot the basement? You'll also have to solve the practical problems of moisture and ventilation before choosing from a beautiful array of ceiling, wall, and floor alternatives.

LEFT **With a little effort, you can hide all telltale signs of a base-ment and ceate livable space.**

easy
solutions

Eyesores such as heating and cooling units can be easily closeted behind doors. You can also conceal intrusive water and gas pipes and heating ducts with a drop ceiling. Or you can add architectural interest and remove pipes from view by hiding them under a coffered ceiling and beams. If you want to impart a utilitarian openness to the space, leave the basement ceiling exposed and paint the pipes, wires, joists, and the underside of the upstairs subfloor one color. Even those ugly metal posts can be hidden in a closet or wall or encased in the frame of a doorway. Or sheath them in a wooden or drywall box. Finish off the box with a moisture-resistant composite material.

ABOVE A decorative screen can hide poles and divide a basement into two areas.

LEFT A terraced window well opens up a basement to more natural light and better ventilation.

OPPOSITE TOP Hide eyesores such as oil tanks, pipes, and heaters with bifold doors.

OPPOSITE BOTTOM Tuck appliances inside cabinets with retractable doors for easy access.

RADON Detection kits that measure radon gas in your basement are sold in many stores. Always follow directions to the letter, and call a radon technician if the kit reveals high levels of this dangerous gas. Solutions usually range from sealing cracks and joints between floors and walls to installing fans and ducts that vent old air to the outside and introduce fresh air into the space. (New materials on the market not only seal out radon but waterproof at the same time.)

ASBESTOS You'll find asbestos typically insulating furnaces or wood-burning stoves or located inside the ductwork in basements. If asbestos doesn't have tears, abrasions, or water damage, it usually releases few dangerous particles that can harm lungs and is best left alone. If you detect damaged asbestos, however, hire a professional to test it and, if necessary, seal, cover, or remove it from your house.

MOISTURE AND AIR QUALITY

MOISTURE Drying out a basement can be as simple as cleaning clogged gutters, regrading a slope away from the foundation, or sealing cracks in the floor and walls and applying a waterproofing medium to them. On the other hand, more-serious moisture problems may require excavating around the exterior foundation and waterproofing the walls and installing a sump pump or a dehumidifier.

POOR VENTILATION Reduce dead air by installing windows, ceiling fans, and even a quiet but powerful exhaust fan with an adjustable gooseneck to displace high levels of heat and humidity.

MOLD Applying a 50-percent solution of laundry bleach and water to affected areas usually kills mold. However, if mold has gotten into rugs and insulation, you may have to replace them.

surfaces
with style

To make your basement livable and give it style, you'll want to finish the ceiling, walls, and floors attractively. There are a number of ways to do this.

CEILINGS TO LOOK UP TO

New technologies have produced a host of durable materials at affordable prices. White flat ceilings are fine, but you might want to consider other options.

DROP CEILINGS Also called suspended ceilings, they hide exposed floor joists, ductwork, and plumbing and wiring. The system includes a framework of

metal channels that hang on wires attached directly to the joists. Drop ceilings automatically create a flat, level ceiling and offer convenient access to electrical and plumbing systems in case of a problem or emergency. Adding insulation to the panels will enhance their acoustic properties.

DRYWALL You can box in pipes and ducts, or create coffered or tray ceilings with drywall. Install fiberglass-batt insulation between the drywall and the floor joists to increase energy efficiency and add sound-proofing. Paint it, and add molding for extra style.

LAMINATE Moisture-resisitant wood-laminate ceilings come prefinished in several colors. They install easily over joists or wood furring strips.

REFLECTIVE CEILINGS Mirrored-acrylic sheets can be installed in a grid that is attached to the joists. A reflective ceiling can make a room feel larger.

OPPOSITE TOP This starry ceiling pattern blends into the wall border where faux tassles accentuate framed ephemera.

OPPOSITE BOTTOM A monochromatic scheme for the walls and ceiling "heightens" the space. Molding adds decorative finesse.

LEFT A lavish treatment on the ceiling and walls of this home theater resembles a European opera house.

ABOVE A painted-ceiling design was inspired by the curlicues in an iron bed's canopy.

DEHUMIDIFIERS

It's not rocket science. Dehumidifiers remove humidity from the air. What can be challenging is purchasing the right-size machine to do the job. Units are rated by how many pints of water per hour—usually 25, 40, or 50—they can remove from the air. To determine your needs, multiply the length and width of your room to figure out the square footage. A 25-pint machine can service most basements of 500 to 2,000 square feet that are moderately or very damp. You'll probably need a 40- or 50-pint machine for 2,500 square feet or more.

More tips for using a dehumifier:

- To save energy, look for automatic models that shut off once a preset level of humidity is reached.
- Buy a machine that allows you to drain the water through a hose or tube directly into a floor drain or sump pump.
- For top efficiency, close doors and windows to make sure fresh, humid air doesn't flow into the basement while your dehumidifier is running.
- In warmer climates, consider dehumidiying a basement with a window- or wall-mounted air-conditioner instead of a dehumidifier, which adds heat to an already-warm space.

FINISHING IDEAS FOR FABULOUS-LOOKING WALLS

These days it is easy to hide those ugly poured-concrete or stacked concrete block foundation walls behind any number of manmade or natural materials that will enhance the look and livability of the room. After any moisture problems are rectified and insulation is added, there is no limit to the style you can achieve.

PAINT AND WALLPAPER

Perhaps the first choice for many people, paint is an inexpensive way to add color. Wallpaper styles are available to suit any taste or function. Use warm whites or reflective wallpaper to amplify limited natural light. Try a vertically striped wallpaper or painted effect to draw the eye up in a room. Use vibrant colors to create excitement in otherwise boring spaces.

BRICK OR STONE VENEER This will add a rustic look to a basement, or it can function as an attractive fireproof backing for a wood-burning stove. Solid stone and brick are heavy and may require additional support. New cast-stone products, which imitate real stone and brick, are thinner, weigh less, and are easy to install.

GLASS BLOCKS Create a nonload-bearing partition wall with glass blocks to reconfigure a space or to add curves

LEFT Creating a perfect arrangement of art on a wall doesn't always require a trained eye. This wallpaper pattern does it for you.

OPPOSITE TOP A deep color looks rich on this wall and provides an excellent backdrop for the artwork.

OPPOSITE Beadboard paneling can be painted or stained. A mellow wood finish adds warmth to this dining area.

MOVE OVER DRYWALL: NEW MATERIALS FOR BASEMENT WALLS

Drywall is a misnomer when it comes to basements with lingering moisture or dampness. Over the years, it remains anything but dry. The building industry has developed solutions to counter persistent moisture problems. Here are some of the newest:

- Better living through chemistry. A new wallboard looks just like typical drywall except that it is impregnated with a biocide that kills mold before it can form on any part of the material—face, core, or back. The downside is that it costs twice as much as regular drywall.
- Inorganic materials. Another new type of wallboard was recently introduced. Its surface and core are made of inorganic glass fibers that resist both mold and mildew.
- Prefabricated wall systems. New all-in-one basement walls, complete with a choice of moldings that snap into place, meet all the challenges that a basement throws at them. Installed directly in front of foundation walls, the wall system resists mold and mildew with durable panels that breathe. The manmade material also resists dents and damage from playful children and adults. In addition, the prefabricated walls are energy efficient, have built-in soundproofing, and can be removed to get access to wiring or foundation walls.

to a boxy room. Construct a half-wall to provide privacy without completely closing off a space. Glass-block walls will allow light to stream from one room into another.

SHEET AND WOOD PANELING Paneling is no longer restricted to the knotty-pine planks of the 1950s rec room. You can find real-wood veneers or real-wood tongue-and-groove paneling that come prefinished or ready for a color or stain of your choice.

CODE CHECKS

As you design your new living space, be sure that it meets the recently modified International Residential Code. For example, the code mandates room height. In habitable spaces—those rooms for living, sleeping, eating, and cooking—the ceiling must be no less than 7 feet high. Ceilings in non-habitable rooms can be 4 inches lower, with beams, girders, and other projections yielding a clearance of no less than 6 feet, 4 inches.

There are codes for other areas, as well. Check before you build.

- Floor space: Habitable rooms must measure at least 7 x 7 feet.

- Kitchens and baths: Check. Both have a long list of codes that must be met.

- Stairs: Check codes for tread, riser, headroom measurements, plus handrail shape and location.

STYLES THAT WILL FLOOR YOU

These days you can have the same wide range of flooring choices as you do for the rest of your home. Here are some of the most popular ones to consider.

CARPETING A carpet softens the hard concrete slab found in most basements and provides coziness and warmth to your living space. In rooms where you want to confine sound, such as a media room, carpet is indispensable. Some come with an antimicrobial chemical that resists mold and mildew. Others are stain-resistant.

CERAMIC TILE Because basements are always subject to water damage, some designers recommend ceramic-tile floors. However, it is cold underfoot.

OPPOSITE TOP The painted trompe l'oeil surfaces only look like stone.

OPPOSITE BOTTOM This laminate floor resembles ceramic tile.

ABOVE Hardwood is always handsome, but it may need an area rug for total comfort.

RIGHT Carpeting softens a concrete basement floor. A pattern adds style.

LAMINATE Laminate material offers the look of natural wood or stone, but it is resistant to moisture and dampness. It comes in strips or tiles. You can't refinish it like wood, and you will have to replace it when it wears.

HARDWOOD You'll find dozens of finishes and configurations available—strip planks, parquet squares, self-stick squares, as well as prefinished options. Although it adds warmth and is easy underfoot, hardwood is expensive and must be maintained and refinished eventually. Also, it is impractical in damp or wet areas.

RESILIENT VINYL Available in sheets or tiles, resilient vinyl is easy to maintain and is comfortable underfoot. The tiles are easy to install or replace yourself if you have a level floor. Vinyl comes in an almost endless selection of colors and styles, including wood, tile, and faux stone. It is an excellent choice for high-activity rooms or areas that are exposed to water.

CORK Unlike wood and laminate, cork comes with its own built-in cushion and is moisture-resistant. It also absorbs sound. A cork floor requires a polyurethane finish to ease sweeping and mopping, but it can last for decades if properly maintained.

PAINT Painting over concrete is the simplest solution of all when it comes to concrete basement floors. Paint it a solid color or apply a decorative paint finish to create the look of wood or stone or to add a pattern.

basement
amenities

Today's remodeled basements have evolved into living spaces that are as comfortable and full of amenities as your upstairs rooms. Here are some options that can fit into just about any basement to make it more liveable and charming.

DIRECT-VENT GAS FIREPLACES Nothing makes a room feel cozier than a toasty-warm fireplace. Tying into the home's exising gas lines, direct-vent fireplaces vent gases through the above-grade portion of the foundation wall to the outside. Direct-vent gas fireplaces will keep cool basement rooms warm in winter and will even work in the case of electrical failure.

VENTLESS GAS FIREPLACES Efficiency is this fireplace's first and middle name. All the heat produced by a ventless gas fireplace is retained within the house. Most ventless gas fireplaces are required to include an oxygen depletion sensor (ODS), a safety feature that warns if oxygen levels in the room are becoming low. These fireplaces work in the event of power outages.

PORTABLE AIR CONDITIONERS A flexible hose vents the hot exhaust to the outside, usually through a window kit that you attach to a windowsill.

APARTMENT-SIZED APPLIANCES If you want to design a cozy snack area or create a complete kitchen, there are scaled-down appliances that can easily fit into small areas—everything from 21-inch-wide stoves to 8.6-cubic-foot refrigerators and mini-dishwashers. Check out modular (and expensive) drawer-size models.

OPPOSITE A traditional masonry fireplace, with a stone face and carved wood mantel and surround, has romantic old-fashioned appeal.

TOP RIGHT Countertop appliances are perfect in a small kitchen. Some of them are so good-looking, you'll want them on display.

RIGHT A direct-vent gas fireplace is an attractive and efficient amenity you may want to include in your remodeled basement room.

basement business

STORAGE SOLUTIONS

It's a fact: living space requires storage space. Don't commit every square foot of your basement to living area without planning adequate storage areas to accommodate it. Here are some ideas.

Make use of the area under the stairs. Often forgotten about and rarely used, the space under the stairs can be fashioned into a cabinet with doors or a hidden library or office supply area with drawers or files that can be rolled out and pulled into view only when you need them.

Install storage along the foundation walls. Because basements tend to be long, running the length of the house, a standard solution is to devote one wall to a series of closets that can house everything from out-of-season clothes to sporting equipment. Use every inch of vertical space when planning shelving. When outfitted with wood-louver doors that allow

air to circulate, closets look good, too. When buying a shelving system, choose one that is adjustable so that you can reconfigure the shelves as your needs change.

Create a storage room. Instead of using valuable wall space in a small basement, design a storage room that will hold absolutely all of your stuff.

Use furniture that is convertible or can be stored when it is not in use. For example, you can expand the size of a small bedroom by installing a wall bed, called a Murphy bed. It neatly folds up into a closet during the day when you aren't sleeping and conveniently drops down when you are ready to turn in for the night. In other parts of the basement, lightweight stackable or fold-up tables and chairs take up little space in the closet or garage can be handy when you entertain.

BELOW Utilize the dead areas under the staircase by installing built-in drawers.

RIGHT An intelligent storage system can be organized with hanging racks and boxes.

OPPOSITE A wall shelving unit can be used as both a bookcase and a showcase.

SMART TIP

In basements with a low ceiling, use horizontal design elements to emphasize the length and width of a room. Set floor tiles in a diagonal pattern. Also, make use of tall vertical elements, such as columns or bookshelves to add the illusion of height. Above all, paint the ceiling a light color.

windows
and doors

Be honest. When you think of basement windows and doors, what probably comes to mind is the lack of choice. The variety of stylish windows and doors available these days will turn that kind of thinking on its head. A new generation of window wells goes beyond those old gray steel versions of yesterday, too. Now you can install window wells that feature French doors opening onto a small patio. Or you can create a gardenlike, outdoorsy feeling by installing greenhouse windows over a basement bumpout.

LEFT Make your remodeled basement bright and airy with the new generation of windows and doors.

windows and doors

Designers and homeowners agree that the last thing anyone wants is a remodeled basement that looks and feels like, well, a basement. So pull out all of the stops when you're choosing windows and doors—which are the sole conduits of natural ventilation and light in your new space.

Even wood doors perform well in the basement, provided that the space is dry and moisture is controlled. So consider making the passage from one area into another outstanding by installing a door that has style. For example, use French doors, which separate without closing off natural light. Try graceful louver doors to house a laundry center or a closet. In a walkout basement, bring the garden inside with large sliding doors and perhaps an eyebrow window over them, if the ceiling is high enough to allow it.

OPPOSITE The entry to an elaborate home theater is as dramatic as the rest of the room thanks to a set of French doors that have been dressed with plush velvet curtains. Tassel tiebacks hold the panels back so that the doors can be opened easily.

RIGHT Even a below-grade room can be filled with natural light. Operable units also maximize the ventilation in the space. Besides, residential building codes require windows of a specific size for certain rooms, even those in a basement.

a world of windows

When remodeling your basement, whether it is a walkout space or one that is a standard below-grade type, you can install new larger windows or additional small windows. You can cut into the wall to add a full-size window or dig down to drop in a large window complete with a sunny well. Homeowners who have a walkout basement with one wall above grade can double or triple their natural light and ventilation by bumping out the wall to create a sunroom.

Install basement windows on the south-facing side of the house to gather maximum sunlight during winter months. But don't forget to factor in privacy, not just aesthetics and light. Avoid placing windows close to sidewalks or neighboring houses. Today's window styles are innumerable. You can mix and match them to maximize ventilation and natural light, and to suit any type of architecture. However, if you plan to install windows in an area that is prominent and visible from the outside, choose a style that blends with the other windows of the house.

CODE CHECKS

Popping in any old basement window and hoping that it meets the building code could cause you headaches later. Be sure to meet window codes, which have been spelled out in the new International Residential Code (IRC), completed in 2000. Here are a few examples.

- In habitable rooms—those used for living, sleeping, eating, or cooking—windows must equal 8 percent of the room's size (in square feet). What's more, half of that window area (also in square feet) must be operable for ventilation or egress. So in other words, in a 100-square-foot room (one that measures 10 x 10 feet) there must be 8 square feet of windows, of which 4 square feet must be operable.
- All sleeping rooms, above or below grade, are required to have either a door to the outside or an egress window with 5.7 square feet of operable area through which a person can exit. Note: some casement and other single-sash windows may not be large enough to meet code requirements.
- Window wells that are 44 inches or more below grade are required to have a permanent ladder or stairs for making an emergency escape.

DOUBLE- AND SINGLE-HUNG Two related types of windows, double- and single-hung windows, are the most common ones found in homes. A double-hung window has a pair of movable sash that slide vertically within the window frame. A single-hung unit has two sash, but only the lower one is operable; the top sash remains in a fixed position.

There are a number of ways to dress up these windows. For instance, manufacturers offer several styles of permanent or snap-in muntins, or grilles, that can be attached on the inside and the outside of the window to create a true divided-light look. You can easily pop out the snap-in grilles for easy window cleaning. What's more, you can purchase double-hung units with sash that tilt inward, so you can clean both sides of the glass from the inside of the house.

It's easy to add even more personality to simple double-hung windows by framing them with one of a number of interior and exterior trim designs, from contemporary to Mission-style. Besides the obvious eye appeal that trim provides, it can make a modest-sized window appear larger. It also gives your basement a finished look that matches the architecture of the house.

CASEMENT The casement-style window features a single sash that is hinged vertically to open out (or sometimes in) by means of a crank. A casement window can be used alone, in pairs within a single frame, or in combination with a fixed window. It provides generous ventilation because the entire sash swings open. New options include collapsible or low-profile crank handles that don't protrude through blinds or get in the way of some other window treatment. You

can dress up casement windows with snap-in grilles, as well. Casement and other single-sash windows may sometimes pose a problem meeting codes. See "Code Checks" on page 35.

AWNING Like a casement window, an awning window is a single-sash design that has a crank, but the unit is hinged on the top. Because this type of window pivots outward horizontally, it can shed rain and still provide ventilation. See "Code Checks."

HOPPER A hopper is the window that is typically associated with a basement. It is hinged at the bottom and tilts in when it is open. A latch at the top will keep it in place when you want the window to remain closed. See "Code Checks."

GLIDER Also called a slider, a glider has two sash set into a track within one frame. For ventilation, the outer sash slides in front of the inner one, which may or may not be fixed. Gliders come in standard sizes but can also be as small as a transom. See "Code Checks."

RIGHT Shutters with operable louvers let you control the amount of light and air that enters a room.

GLASS BLOCK If security is an issue, glass-block windows might be an option in some areas of a remodeled basement, provided you have other windows that meet IRC egress and ventilation codes. They discourage burglaries because the glass is impact-resistant. These days, lightweight acrylic or vinyl "glass-block" windows also come in operable casement, awning, and hopper styles. Clear glass blocks provide an unobstructed view. For privacy, you can install glass-block panels, with or without air vents, that have prismatic, undulated, and non-directional patterns.

WINDOW WELLS: DIGGING DEEP FOR NATURAL LIGHT

Below-grade windows can let in as almost as much light as their aboveground cousins, thanks to a new generation of window wells that seamlessly combine function and design. While traditional steel wells have been a popular choice in the past, homeowners are embracing fiberglass and high-density polyethylene models in a variety of contemporary colors (warm whites and neutrals) and much larger sizes. New window wells can accommodate 4-, 5-, and even 6-foot-wide picture windows.

Although wells deeper than 44 inches are required by code to have steps or a ladder for escape in case of an emergency, they don't have to look, well, ugly. Window wells with steps, for instance, can be transformed into gardens by planting your favorite plants and flowers in them. Some wells can be finished with the same siding as the house to maintain a consistent look. Several companies manufacture window well panels with highly realistic eye-popping scenes of mountains and oceans that can be inserted right over your present window well to open up vistas.

LIGHT-SCATTERING WELL Still another trend is a window well that doesn't just passively conduct light into a basement. Instead it captures the sunshine that hits the foundation and siding above the well and projects it across the ceiling and into rooms. A light-scattering window well reflects 10 times more natural light into a basement than traditional models.

ABOVE A window well with a stepped-terrace design provides an emergency escape from a basement. This one also features a visually pleasing place for growing plants.

GREENHOUSE WINDOWS: THE EFFECT IS BRILLIANT

You don't have to be an avid gardener to want greenhouse windows installed in your new basement—just someone who wants to light up the remodeled space with sunlight. Greenhouse units come as a single window with shelves for plants or an entire unit that runs the width of the house. In a walkout basement, you can install a greenhouse unit across the length of the entry. In a standard basement, you can excavate an area and install a unit complete with a patio and garden.

The view and the extra light afforded by greenhouse units are especially helpful in a hobby or craft studio and inspiring in a home gym, where the motivation to work out is sometimes difficult to summon. To maximize the natural light from greenhouse windows, be sure to install French doors or any other style of glass doors in contiguous rooms to let the light wash through your space.

doors for
every room

Once upon a time, wood doors weren't considered a sensible option for basement rooms. With more-efficient dehumidifiers and ample ventilation from larger basement windows and ceiling fans, even wood doors have a home down below. In fact, according to designers, the mantra is what works upstairs most likely will work downstairs.

Your choice depends on the function of the room and the effect you are trying to create in your newly remodeled space. If cost is a concern, you might think about composite doors made of plastic and wood rather than wood. The downside is that composite doors can only be painted, not stained (although you can paint them with a faux-wood finish).

STYLE FACTORS Although there are no hard-and-fast rules about decorating, it's usually a good idea to match the style of any door with the rest of the house. At the very least, keep the door styles consistent in the basement. If that's not possible or if you're recycling doors from other areas in the house, ways to link mismatched doors include painting or staining them all the same color and installing similar hardware. Paying attention to these details will make the difference in the finished result. For example a brushed-nickel knob or lever will look out of place on a door with brass hinges, while thick doors can impart a sense of luxury. Arch-shaped doors or ones upholstered in fabric or decorated with trompe l'oeil will alert visitors that they are entering a special space, such as a wine cellar or a cigar room.

WHAT'S FUNCTIONING Sometimes the purpose of the room will dictate your choice. A door to a home workshop should have a tight seal in order to keep fumes and dust from spreading to living or sleeping areas.

French doors usually aren't the best option when you want to close off a room that's cluttered with sewing projects, for example. On the other hand, glass doors are an excellent way to divide basement space because they allow natural light to pass from a bright room into one that is dark. Glass entry doors can extend the sense of spaciousness, as well.

OPPOSITE The right style door and its finish can play up a particular decorating scheme, such as Mediterranean style.

BELOW Glass doors will allow light to pass through adjoining areas. Use them to brighten a windowless space by borrowing sunlight from another room.

ENERGY STAR: PANES WITH A PURPOSE

By some estimates, a house loses one-fifth of its total energy through basement walls, windows, and doors. Here are some clear choices to help cut your energy costs.

■ Double-pane windows. Most all good-quality windows today are fitted with insulated glass. This means the glazing is a sandwich of two panes of glass separated by warm channel spacers. The spacers keep the exchange of inside and outside temperatures to a minimum. Not surprisingly, double-pane windows are twice as efficient as single-pane ones and can keep your energy bill down.

■ Triple-pane windows. As you would expect, these windows have three glass layers, but they are not that much more efficient than double-pane windows, although they are considerably heavier and more costly to install.

■ Argon-filled glass. Providing energy efficiency similar to that of triple-pane glass, some double-pane windows use argon gas instead of air between the two panes of glass.

■ Low-e glass. Coated with a microscopic layer of silver and metal oxides, low-emissivity (low-e) glass permits 75 percent of visible light to pass through but reduces heat transfer, helping to keep your basement warmer in winter and cooler in summer. Double-pane windows with low-e coating are more energy efficient and less expensive overall than triple-pane windows.

wíndows and doors

SMART TIP

To save floor space in a small room, such as a bathroom or bedroom, consider installing a pocket door (below), which slides sideways into the wall.

EXTERIOR DOORS

A common choice in a walkout basement is a sliding glass-door unit on a track. It lets maximum light into the living space. However, hinged glass doors will admit as almost much light They have tighter seals, and they will cut down on energy bills. Hinged doors also come in a variety of styles—from French to Mission-style to contemporary.

BULKHEAD DOORS In a standard basement without an exterior entrance, bulkhead doors—the sloping metal doors that open up from both sides and cover a below-grade stairway into the basement—aren't as handsome as above-grade doors, but they do make the space accessible from the outside. They are helpful for getting into a workshop and for accommodating large items, such as patio furniture, in and out of storage. Newer models not only have slide-bolt locks but may come with a keyed lock kit that can be set from the outside.

ABOVE An exterior door like this one can be used at the bottom of a cellar stairway that is reached through bulkhead doors.

play it safe

As any local police department will tell you, first-floor and basement windows and doors are prime entries for burglars. While wiring windows and doors with a home anti-theft system is a smart move, there are additional options, short of installing security bars. Here are a few of them.

LAMINATED GLASS Made with a durable plastic inner layer, laminated glass, which can be used in doors as well as windows, is difficult to break. It has become an increasingly popular choice for people who are concerned about basement security.

IMPACT-RESISTANT GLASS Originally designed to stand up against hurricane-force wind, impact-resistant glass is also effective for home security because a burglar will not be able to break it, even with a 2x4 piece of wood. However, a window made with impact-resistant glass is expensive, costing about 30 percent more than a window made of standard glass.

WINDOW PINS AND ANTI-SLIDING DEVICES You can reinforce the closure on a wooden double-hung window by inserting a device called a window pin into the upper sash. The pin can prevent the sash from opening even if the glass is broken. You can insert a wooden dowel into the track of a sliding glass door or window, but various track blockers and anti-sliding devices can secure them more effectively by making it impossible for an intruder to lift the unit out of the track.

BRING IN THE SUNSHINE

To brighten and increase the airiness of your basement, here are some design tricks to enhance the natural light, no matter how much you get.

- Color. Painting the walls a warm neutral or warm white (below) and installing light-color carpeting, vinyl, or wood flooring considerably amplify natural light.
- Furnishings. Wicker or rattan furniture or tables with glass tops, as well as other furnishings that are open and light-friendly, add airiness and a free-flowing feeling to an otherwise drab space.
- Reflective surfaces. Install mirrors and other reflective materials (right) that can bounce natural or artificial light back into a room

turn on the light

L ighting is one of the most important design elements in any room. It is critical in a basement, where natural light is often at a premium. Coordinating all of your artificial lighting sources—lamps, recessed or track lighting, sconces, ceiling-mounted fixtures, even pendants—can make the difference between a place that is warm and welcoming or one that is dark and depressing. In addition, light can be used in more focused ways—whether that be illuminating a work surface or minimizing reflection as you watch TV.

LEFT Candlelight is the perfect way to enhance the mood of a basement room that's meant for relaxing.

plan for lighting

Your new basement living space should probably combine varying amounts of ambient, task, and accent lighting. The way you plan to use the room will determine how much you'll need of each of these three types. If you're putting together a workshop or craft room, you'll need good task lighting. For a home theater or media room, soft ambient lighting will serve you well. For displaying a collection, focused accent lighting is desirable. Don't forget: light also has the power to visually reconfigure space, making your belowground rooms seem larger, for example. Play other tricks with light: shine attention on architectural high points or obscure less desirable details. Try bulbs of different wattage until you find your comfort level.

ABOVE Comtemporary lighting fixtures, such as these, are affordable and can bring a lot of style into a room.

RIGHT The combination of several types of lighting looks sophisticated in this basement-bar area.

SMART TIP

If you have installed dimmers, you can dim lights just slightly to extend lamp life and save energy, and there will be very little perceptible change in light level. For instance, dimming the light to 50 percent will be perceived as though the light were only dimmed to 70 percent. Therefore, there is no dramatic dilation or constriction of the eye due to light level change.

Also, you can avoid eyestrain by having plenty of ambient light, thereby reducing the contrast to task lighting. In addition, the lighting level depends on the activity and its intensity. For example, reading for a short period of time typically requires less-intense task lighting than reading for an extended amount of time.

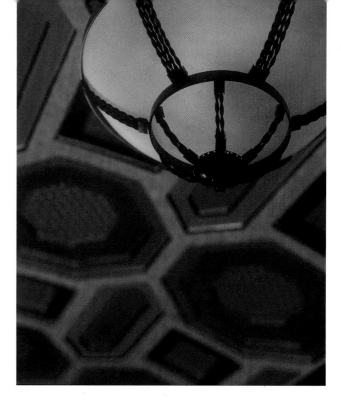

AMBIENT LIGHT

Because this is the overall light that fills a room, ambient light is also called general light. Obviously, it is critical to the mood of a room and its function. Because natural light can be scarce or nonexistent in a basement, you will have to compensate with artificial light. Today you can find fixtures for coordinating your lighting needs with any decorating style, but some are functionally more suitable for particular situations.

FIXTURES Standard ceiling-mounted fixtures, such as fluorescent strips and recessed canisters, are typical choices for ambient light. Downlights, pendants and chandeliers can be fine for general lighting, but usually direct light upward, where it washes the wall and is reflected back into the room.

Other possible sources of good general lighting are lamps with opaque shades. But the important thing to remember is that ambient light is inconspicuous. Although you know the source of the light, the glow is diffused. Of course, never use an exposed bulb, which is much too harsh.

LIGHT LEVELS How bright should you make the room, or how much ambient light should you plan for your new basement space? That all depends on the particular room and the atmosphere that you want. To create the precise level of light, wire ambient light sources to dimmer switches. This puts you in control and allows you to easily adjust the light depending on your mood, the time of day, and the activity. For example, you will want subdued lighting for watching a movie, general lighting for household tasks, and stronger, more cheerful lighting when you're hosting a kid's birthday party or entertaining friends.

OPPOSITE A floor lamp with a paper shade provides diffused light. The fixture's interesting shape makes it a piece of art, as well.

ABOVE Reproduction fixtures, like this ceiling fixture, can make a home theater look like an old movie house.

LEFT Sleek understated style makes this sconce the perfect accent in a contemporary bathroom.

turn on the light

TASK LIGHTING

This kind of lighting focuses on a specific area. It illuminates the work surface—whether it be the top of your desk in a home office or a work table in a workshop— not the room. Metal architects' lamps, under-cabinet lights, reading lamps, and desk lamps are all excellent examples of task lighting. Optimally, task lights should be angled between you and the work. A reading lamp functions best, after all, when it is positioned behind you and over your shoulder. Aiming light directly on a surface creates glare, which causes eye strain.

If part of your basement remodeling will include a bathroom, you should include task lights for grooming.

SHADE STRATEGIES

You can detract from a lighting scheme or even ruin the room's decor if you use the wrong lamp shade. Here's what you should know.

- Translucent shades diffuse or filter light for a warm glow in a window or as welcoming beacon and focal point in a large dark room.
- Opaque shades allow light to escape only from the top and bottom. The shades offer drama and won't reflect back at you from the windows at nighttime or from the television screen in a media room.
- Paper shades with gold lining will provide a special golden glow. Use them on candle sconces for an extra special accent, but not for truly functional illumination.

OPPOSITE LEFT
Side sconces are excellent for task-lighting a bathroom mirror. Overhead lights can cast unflattering shadows.

OPPOSITE RIGHT A gooseneck desk lamp is a classic. Don't place it where it can be reflected in a computer screen.

RIGHT A fan-shaped sconce focuses light on the ceiling, creating a dramatic mood in a home theater.

SMART TIP

The darker the room, the more supplemental light you will need. Dark walls eat up light while light-colored tones reflect and amplify it.

ACCENT LIGHTING

Designers like to use accent lighting because it is decorative and often dramatic. Accent lighting draws attention to a favorite work of art, a recessed niche on a stairway landing, a tall plant at the end of a long room, or a collection of favorite sports memorabilia or awards inside a cabinet. However, when using accent lighting, be sure the source is concealed in order not to detract from what you hope to highlight.

Small spotlights called "eyeballs" are excellent fixtures for accenting art or interesting architectural features. You can aim them directly at anything. Use low-voltage halogen bulbs, which won't get too hot.

OPPOSITE Eyeball spotlights mounted under the cabinets accentuate the art on the wall and create the sense of a niche within two tall units.

ABOVE RIGHT Direct accent lighting over a priceless artpiece, combined with recessed light, can bring an overflowing amount of drama to a basement dining area.

RIGHT Cove lighting adds a decorative accent in this room. Recessed downlights accentuate the art and wash the walls for more drama.

LEFT Wall sconces provide accent lighting that complements the overall scheme in this room.

BOTTOM An opaque shade on a table lamp diffuses the light to a welcoming glow.

OPPOSITE TOP LEFT Well-placed recessed fixtures light this basement play area evenly.

OPPOSITE FAR RIGHT A torchère is a stylish source of portable, supplemental lighting for a TV or family room.

OPPOSITE BOTTOM LEFT A candle sconce is a pretty way to light a hallway.

FIXTURE FACTS

There are many styles and shapes of light fixtures from which to choose. Match your choice with your needs.

- Pendants hang from the ceiling and can direct light upward or downward. Use them for general lighting.
- Chandeliers are a type of pendant with "branches" that extend in many directions to disperse light evenly, not just down onto the table. The more branches a chandelier has, the more light it produces. To answer an age-old question: there should be 30 to 34 inches between the bottom of the fixture and the top of the table.
- Sconces are wall-mounted fixtures that can face toward the ceiling or down toward a work surface. Use them for accent or general lighting.
- Torchères are tall floor lamps that resemble torches. They diffuse light or direct it upward. Use for general lighting.
- Track lights are focused lamps that are on a wall- or ceiling-mounted track. Use for accent lighting.
- Recessed lights have canister-style housing for bulbs. They are recessed into the ceiling. Use them for general lighting. Eyeball fixtures are similar, but they are adjustable and allow you to angle light in any direction. Use them to accent areas or "wash" walls or objects.

bulb
enlightenment

Y ou can "paint" your basement rooms with light through several means: the angle from which you direct the light, the brightness or intensity of the bulb, and color. You need one kind of lighting plan for a hallway through which you pass quickly and another for a family room where you will typically camp out for hours. Using the right type of bulb is important.

Ideally, artificial light should imitate natural light as closely as possible. Becoming familiar with the characteristics of the different types of bulbs will help you to light your new space properly.

ABOVE Use lighting inside glass-door cabinets. Under cabinet lights are perfect for illuminating countertop tasks.

RIGHT Keep the lighting soft in a room that's intended for sleeping or relaxing.

INCANDESCENT BULBS

These are the standard bulbs with which you are probably familiar. Invented by Thomas Edison, the incandescent bulb is the type that you have undoubtedly used in table and floor lamps or overhead fixtures, including chandeliers, many times. Incandescent lighting provides a warm, cozy glow that accentuates reds and yellows in a decorating scheme and is generally flattering to you and your interiors. But these bulbs get hot and may not be the most energy-efficient choice for a confined space such as a compact home office or recessed under cabinets in the kitchen or workshop. In addition, traditional incandescents burn out more quickly than other types of bulbs. There are improved longer-lasting versions today, however, as well as ones that burn whiter, more natural light.

SMART TIP

Because eyes are drawn to the bright objects, you can "extend" a smaller room in a walkout basement by placing a bright accent light in the garden or patio just outside the glass doors. The garden or patio will magically become a part of the room.

LOW-VOLTAGE HALOGENS

These are actually a type of incandescent bulb that run on 12 volts of electricity. They are smaller and run more efficiently than their standard incandescent counterparts, although they are higher priced. Halogens also produce a whiter, more natural-looking light than other types of bulbs. Most contemporary designs use low-voltage halogens as task lighting in the form or small spotlights or as strips under shelves or within cabinets, or as ambient lighting in pendants, chandeliers, and wire systems because they are compact.

FLUORESCENT BULBS

These bulbs last 10 times as long and produce considerably more light per watt than a standard incandescent bulb. However, standard fluorescent lights are cold and and render light that is predominantly blue. You can't put fluorescent bulbs on a dimmer switch, either. However, newer versions of the fluorescent bulb (called "deluxe warm white") have eliminated some of the older type's liabilities, thankfully, because fluorescent light has its uses in some workshops or in closets. The improved fluorescent is similar in color to an incandescent bulb.

ABOVE LEFT Compact low-voltage halogen spotlights illuminate a trio of bookcases.

ABOVE RIGHT Overhead fixtures provide an abundant amount of light in a home office.

LEFT Pendant lights that hang low from the ceiling, combined with recessed lighting fixtures, bring out the bright colors of this game room. Invite some friends over on a Saturday night and enjoy a few games of pool.

OPPOSITE TOP This home exercise room uses track lighting to accentuate the equipment. After the workout and a long shower, the well-lit mirror is handy for grooming.

OPPOSITE BOTTOM In addition to general lighting, this home office also has an adjustable-arm desk lamp that is aimed away from the computer screen to avoid eyestraining glare.

lighting solutions: room by room

With lighting, one size doesn't fit all. Each room presents its own lighting challenges and solutions. Think outside of the box. Recessed lighting, for example, can be tucked away under bookshelves, not just in the ceiling; track lighting can be installed in a circular pattern to mirror a room with sweeping curves rather than in straight strips. Here are some other strategies for lighting each of your new basement rooms.

FAMILY/PLAY ROOM Install a handsome ceiling-mounted fixture in the center of the room to create balance and interest. Add recessed lighting in the corners or near doors and windows. Or if the room is designed for active play, plan for recessed lighting throughout. If you need light in the center of the room, install floor outlets.

MEDIA/TV ROOM No light should be brighter than the TV screen. Three-way bulbs or dimmers are often the best solution. Remember: keep the light behind you.

HOME OFFICE Use an adjustable desktop lamp to focus light on the task at hand and to deflect glare from a computer screen.

STAIRCASE You will need at least one 60-watt fixture per 10 feet of stairs. Try recessed lighting in the ceiling, or install lighting in several recessed out-of-the-way niches along the staircase wall.

KITCHEN Team up general illumination with under-the-cabinet task lighting for food preparation. A good plan might include recessed or ceiling-mounted fixtures that are installed about 12 to 15 inches from the front of the upper cabinets and a another one or two fixtures over the sink. Interior cabinet lighting is attractive, especially if there are glass doors. Don't forget to add task lighting. Try compact fluorescent or halogen strips that can be mounted under wall cabinets. If the ceiling height permits, pendants are a stylish option over a kitchen island or peninsula or above the table.

BEDROOM Any number of lighting combinations could work in a bedroom, but generally an overhead fixture that you flip on when you first

SMART TIP

Use a fluorescent fixture in the workshop.

enter the room is practical. For a more intimate mood, wiring bedside lamps to a light switch will also work. A must-have is a swing-arm reading lamp with a narrow beam of light that enables you to finish your novel while allowing your spouse to catch up on shuteye.

BATHROOM As with a home office, you need ambient (general) light that helps you find your way to the toilet or shower without tripping and task lighting for personal grooming. The ideal task lighting should come from both sides of the mirror at eye level and should be equidistant from the mirror.

HOME WORKSHOP A workable solution that has stood the test of time is fluorescent fixtures at regular intervals along the ceiling and work lights for specific tasks. Installing outlet strips on the wall behind the work surface will let you plug in portable lights when needed.

media rooms: get wired

W hen it comes to the basement, a remodeler's first inclination is often to carve out space for a media room. That's a smart move, as it turns out. An entertainment room outfitted with one or more video-game consoles and a big-screen television that pulls in several movie channels and sporting events from around the country taps into a basement's natural assets: darkness, separation from everyday household activities, and shape. Most basements are rectangular, the shape many audio experts recommend for realistic sound.

LEFT An ideal media room is designed with enough space for both comfort and storage.

sublime design

A successor to the low-tech TV room, today's media room can offer a multimedia experience. It can be outfitted with everything from DVD players to sophisticated home theater setups.

Creating a media room in the basement means more than hooking up electronics. You'll need proper housing for all of the components, as well as comfortable furnishings. You can go the custom route, or check out the specialty cabinetry that's on the market. Manufacturers also design movie-house-style row seating complete with cup holders and reclining chaises, and floor-to-ceiling soundproofing systems that help to enhance the rich sound from digital equipment.

When it comes to furniture, the main focus should be on functionality—enhancing your comfort and the entertainment experience. You can achieve both by furnishing the room with chairs, sectionals, and sofas that are upholstered in soft fabrics. Upholstery absorbs sound and can provide the comfort level you need when watching a two-hour movie.

OPPOSITE FAR LEFT
Theater-type recliners, complete with cupholders, transform an ordinary basement into a modern and luxurious media center.

LEFT A freestanding media cabinet can be decorative as well as practical. Solid doors conceal equipment when not in use, and etched side doors accentuate a collection of pottery.

ABOVE This armoire is designed specifically for storing a modest-size TV and a VCR or DVD player. It has drawers for storing DVDs and VHS tapes.

media rooms

CABINETRY AND STORAGE

First, you need space for various components, such as a DVD player, VCR, CD player, and so forth. Next, there's what will indeed be a growing collection of DVDs, videotapes, CDs, and remote controls. If you plan to order custom cabinetry for the space, buy your sound system and home theater components first, then have the cabinetmaker design the unit accordingly.

RIGHT **A storage cabinet with slide-in doors conserves space.**

BELOW **Ready-to-assemble units are an affordable option.**

OPPOSITE **Modular shelving adequately houses audio components.**

In terms of design, the cabinetry should accommodate components at eye level for easy operation. The topmost and lowest shelves can be reserved for lesser-used items. If you'll build the cabinet yourself, remember that there should be enough space around the components to "breathe;" built-in electronics need ventilation. Plus, you have to leave space in the back for wires and plugs, and openings to pull through any wires that have to be plugged into wall outlets.

In addition, be sure to include plenty of rollout drawers in the design to hold your library of favorite discs and tapes. Leave room for future purchases, too. Another option is to store tapes in a closet, a handsome trunk, or even a basket. Stockpiling tapes, CDs, and other clutter around the television screen can detract from the viewing experience.

When not in use, large TV monitors can look like big black ugly boxes. Hide smaller televisions—27- or 32-inch—behind the handsome doors of a semicustom TV cabinet. Very large screens should probably be housed behind pocket, tambour, or concealed doors. Large cabinet doors that swing out into the room can obstruct traffic or even your view of the screen.

Flat-screen TVs have monitors that are only a few inches thick. Their sleek design allows you to enjoy big-screen theater without sacrificing a lot of floor space.

OPPOSITE TOP
Media cabinets come in many popular looks and finishes that coordinate with other furniture. This one has Arts and Crafts styling.

OPPOSITE BOTTOM A flat-screen TV can be mounted on the wall or installed in a cabinet that was designed to accommodate its shape and size.

ABOVE RIGHT
A cabinet that is outfitted with a rollout shelving system is a great way to keep your DVDs and CDs organized.

RIGHT Theater-style seating with built-in drawers provide point-of-use storage for the family's favorite movies.

SMART TIP

Lamps in a media room should have black or dark opaque lampshades that direct light up and down. Translucent shades radiate light in all directions.

ABOVE Dramatic fixtures, accent border lighting, and deep violet colors add drama and flair to the entire basement theater experience.

media-wise moves

No matter the size of your budget or the physical dimensions of your space, there are a full range of options that will make a media room look as good as it sounds. You don't necessarily have to hire a professional or be one yourself to make design decisions that will enhance the space and your use of it.

LIGHTING

Rather than one or two bright-light sources, install several low-level lights. Dimmers will allow you to adjust lights for comfortably viewing a DVD or computer screen or for reading or close-up work. As a general rule, no light should be brighter than the TV screen. Indirect illumination that provides ambient light without on-screen glare is best for a media room. To avoid eyestrain, position light sources behind you and not between you and the screen.

TOP Sconces with low-wattage bulbs are part of an overall lighting scheme that was conceived as an integral part of a professionally designed home theater.

ABOVE In a TV room that's short on space, a leather ottoman doubles as a convenient small table for books, magazines, remote controls, or even a snack tray.

SMART TIP

Odd-shaped rooms — those with more than four walls or an alcove — hold on to sound better than a space with four walls. One easy way to accomplish that is by including bookcases of different widths and heights in the media room. Books help cut down on echo, and the cases themselves break up an evenly dimensioned room — 10 x 12 or 12 x 14 — into an oddly dimensioned space, which provides a richer, more realistic sound.

WALLS, FLOORS, CEILINGS, AND DOORS

Light colored walls will reflect sunlight or artificial light and increase glare, both of which can wash out a television or computer screen. For the same reason, mirrors and other shiny materials or glossy finishes in a media room don't make sense. Choose deep neutrals such as mocha or cappuccino for walls, or even try a darker tone. Walls lined with corkboard, upholstered in fabric, or outfitted with high-tech sound-absorbing glass-fiber panels covered in fashionable fabrics are all good options.

Acoustical ceiling tiles are a simple and effective solution to prevent sound from leaking into upstairs living areas. They come in a range of styles, one of which is bound to fit in with your decor. Double the tiles' sound-proofing properties by first installing fiberglass batts between the floor joists.

Carpeting is not only easy on the feet but also on the ear, preventing harsh echos from bouncing around the room. Hard floor surfaces, such as tile, stone, and marble, can reflect and distort the sound coming from even the most expensive receiver and speakers. Cover the floor in a low-pile, low-maintenance Berber, sisal, or industrial carpet to keep sound true and pure.

When it comes installing an entry door in the media room, some designers recommend a thick, insulated exterior-grade door to keep sound from leaking out. They also suggest an ample-sized entryway so that furniture and large equipment can be brought in easily.

SMART TIP

The media room is not the place for overblown floral prints on fabrics or wallpaper. Nor is it a room that should have a lot of knickknacks. Clutter makes it difficult to focus on the picture. Keep the decorating simple. Create a muted solid-color or small-print background, and eliminate distractions.

OPPOSITE A serious home theater is a luxury that many homeowners are adding to the house, sometimes in the basement. You might incorporate all or some of its features in your media room.

ABOVE Colorful, rich furnishings, plush carpeting, and ornamental lighting enhance this basement living room and create a warm, cozy feeling. Install a chandelier and add a large painting for elegance.

PLUGGING INTO YOUR TV OPTIONS

Technology has clearly taken television to the next level. Even if you have an older standard model, you can improve the picture quality of broadcast viewing simply by adding cable, and even more by adding digital cable or digital satellite.

■ HDTV, or high-definition television, has twice the picture clarity of standard TV, whether you're watching network or cable TV broadcasts or viewing a DVD. Ironically, most HDTVs don't contain high-definition tuners. So, although the picture may be better, you're not getting true HDTV unless you buy the tuning box, which is sold separately and costs around $700. Still, it's an improvement over the old standard versions.

■ Plasma and LCD TV Screens. Thin TV is also a trend that is here to stay. Slimmed down flat-screen plasma TVs and LCD screens provide brilliant colors, better contrast and resolution, and a greater viewing angle. Because the screen is flat, there is no problem with glare. Having the lights on or off does not affect the picture. LCDs are smaller; screens range from 15 to 30 inches diagonally. Plasma TVs start at 32 inches and go up to big-screen size from there. Most of them accept HDTV signals, but they are usually not powerful enough to display all of the high resolution.

■ Rear projection. The screen size of a rear-projection TV is large—40 to 82 inches—and can be viewed in natural light without sacrificing picture quality. In general, the picture is often inferior, unless it is an HDTV format. Another drawback: rear projection TVs must be watched at eye level and straight-on for optimal viewing.

■ Front projection. This system has a separate screen, which can either drop down from the ceiling or remain fixed on the wall, and a projector that is mounted at ceiling height across the room from the screen. (See the projector in the photo, left.) It's akin to a movie-theater system. Front projection is expensive and requires a professional to install it. Although even minor light can wash out the picture, the image quality is unbeatable when the room is dark.

UPGRADING THE HOME THEATER EXPERIENCE

If you're thinking of creating a home theater in your remodeled basement, here are a few pointers.

- Most home-theater designers recommend televisions screens that are at least 27 inches wide.

- Seating distance is important for viewing quality. For optimum viewing, there should be a distance between you and the TV that is 2 to 2½ times the width of the screen. If your TV is a wide-screen high definition TV (HDTV; see the sidebar, "Plugging into Your TV Options," page 73), place a distance that is 1½ times the screen's diagonal width between you and it.

- Five speakers will create a full-home theater sound. Place one speaker on each side of the TV screen, level with your ears when you are seated and about 3 feet from the sidewalls. Place two speakers behind the sofa about 6 to 8 feet off the floor and at least as wide apart as the front speakers. Put the fifth speaker on top of the TV.

OPPOSITE A wide-screen TV, housed in semicustom cabinetry, and a plush wraparound sofa make this media room a complete family living space.

RIGHT Today's home theaters are installed with all the amenities of a real cinema; surround-sound speakers, pendant lighting, and a centered screen for optimum viewing pleasure.

laundry and family rooms

At first glance, pairing these two rooms might seem a little odd, if not mutually exclusive. When you are doing laundry, you're not thinking about recreating with the family, right? Not necessarily. Increasingly, families are opening up their basement floor plan to create a laundry-and-family room suite. And it makes sense when you think about it. Waiting for the washing and drying of clothes leaves plenty of time for working on craft projects, for example, playing with the kids, or keeping an eye on them while accomplishing tasks.

LEFT **Create your own family studio, complete with a laundry center, computer desk, and storage.**

LEFT Maximize space by installing a cabinet for a fold-out ironing board, or go all out with an ironing center. This appliance has an adjustable board, storage for a hot iron, and automatic shutoff controls.

OPPOSITE RIGHT Neatness counts, even in the basement. Keep the accoutrements of TV viewing contained in an entertainment unit that can also store games and has additional nooks for miscellaneous items.

SMART TIP

Use tall plants to tie wall art to nearby furnishings. Connecting wall art to a reference point, such as the architecture or furnishings, integrates the artwork into the overall scheme. In decorating parlance, create line, rhythm, balance, and harmony for a pleasing result.

Designing a family room is one of the easiest conversions for a basement. There are no special considerations such as plumbing, closets, or egress windows. The main issues are keeping the space dry and selecting finishes for walls, floors, and ceilings. A new laundry room is equally easy to plan. A typical laundry hookup requires hot and cold water supply lines and a drain system, items readily accessible in a basement.

SMART MOVES

When planning a family room, keep flexibility in mind. Will the space be used mostly by the kids, or will you entertain there, as well? What will you do with the room when the kids grow up and move out? Modular seating pieces let you rearrange the room as needs change. Portable lighting and freestanding cabinets and shelves can be moved in or out to accommodate new hobbies or living arrangements.

Laundry rooms are becoming like other rooms in the home—multipurpose places. If you have ample space, consider adding an ironing center, a hobby table, or a small desk for working on bills or catching up on correspondence. If you sew, incorporate your machine into the room. Include large wicker baskets or plastic containers to hold your children's playthings, so they can spend time with you as you attend to your your tasks or projects.

Whether you plan to combine these two rooms in your basement renovation or keep them separate, here are more ideas for making them special.

THE "FAMILY STUDIO"

Laundry facilities can be incorporated handsomely into a room in the basement that is designed for a multitude of needs and activities. Stock or semicustom kitchen cabinetry can hide front-loading washers and dryers, hanging racks, ironing equipment, hampers, and laundry products when they are not in use. The illustration, right, shows you one major appliance manufacturer's suggestion for creating a "family studio" outfiited for multi-tasking. It features gym equipment, a TV, and a mini kitchen. You can work out, watch the news, heat up a snack for the kids, or brew a fresh pot of coffee while you're getting the laundry washed, pressed, and organized.

® Stephen Fuller, Inc.

flexible family style

Family rooms are often a hub of different activities all going on at once. Your teenager might be doing her homework on the computer while you curl up with a book and someone else plays videogames. Paying attention to design issues will help you fashion a comfortable, workable room that enhances togetherness. Even a room that will be in the basement can be attractive.

FURNITURE STRATEGIES Plan furniture groupings to encourage both comfort and conversation, but don't crowd too much furniture in a small room, either. Leave enough space for walking around the furniture

or for stretching your legs when you're seated. If the space is large, don't line the perimeter of the room with furniture, leaving a large open space in the middle. Two or more seating areas increases the room's versatility. Group pieces around a fireplace or a TV. Then put a chair or two in a far corner away from the main hub.

Seating should be comfortable, durable—it will see

OPPOSITE BELOW A washable slipcover is always a smart idea. Custom slipcovers can be expensive, but ready-made versions are affordable and now come in a wide range of styles, colors, and prints.

LEFT Create a grouping in front of a major piece of furniture or focal point, such as a wall unit, a fireplace, or a large-screen TV. Ottomans or portable chairs can be pulled into the arrangement when extra seating is needed.

ABOVE Versatile, informal pieces are key in a family room. This coffee table is an excellent example. Put your feet up on it; let the kids color on it; and toss the toys, tapes, and TV listing in the drawers.

a lot of use—and easy-to-clean upholstered pieces. If you have young children, slipcovers are a wise choice. Just remove and throw them into the washer when the inevitable spill or mess happens. Light, casual, touch-able fabrics, such as cotton, denim, and sisal, wear well and welcome family and friends to put their feet up and let their hair down.

A coffee table is a must, providing space for maga-zines, books, and your feet. Choose a table that allows you to adjust its height for different activities, whether it's dining, card-playing, or laptop computing. Glossy surfaces, like glass tabletops, shelves, or cabinets, are probably not a good idea with young children. Finger-prints show up, and accidents happen.

DIVIDING UP THE SPACE If your family room will be divided up into a mini-game room and a TV room, consider using a built-in divider or several bookshelf units placed side by side to provide separation of space and function. Another option is a three-paneled screen with wheels that you can move from one side of the room to another. Think of the divider as more than a barrier and as a great source of storage. Drawers and shelves can hold favorite books and magazines, as well as board games, remotes, and other paraphernalia. Cutouts at the top of the divider can store bowls or baskets and cabinets at each end can display collectibles or other decorative items. Leave open space in the center of the divider to impart an airy feeling and to allow adults to keep an eye on the kids.

You can adapt these ideas for a combined laundry and family room, too. A divider that contains storage space can keep detergents and other laundry-related products out of sight but handy when you need them. If you don't want a built-in piece, you can easily find ready-to-assemble units that will do the job nicely. They are typically inexpensive and take little time and no special skills or tools to put them together.

KEEP IT LIGHT The best family rooms contain natural light by day and provide enough artificial lighting at night to support a range of activities. Planning a family room next to an exterior sliding glass door or double French doors, will make the room brighter and lighter. Also, maximize window area. Egress windows can funnel in sunlight, while artificial sources can illuminate areas with low headroom. Although family rooms often serve as sanctuaries where you can get away from it all, don't seal off the space from the rest of the basement rooms. Try to include open passages or windows that maintain ties to other rooms or to the outdoors.

OPPOSITE A large-screen TV is often an important feature in a family gathering spot.

RIGHT Extra pillows with removeable, washable covers are great accents.

FAR RIGHT If possible, keep the layout open. Encase support poles in prefabricated decorative columns to divide basement spaces stylishly.

RIGHT Choose casual funiture and low-maintenance materials.

SMART TIP

You'll have to use waterproof flooring material in the laundry area, but you'll want something soft underfoot in the lounging area. Coordinate them by matching the colorways and avoiding bold patterns.

the laundry: a clean, well-lighted place

There was a time when the location of a washer and dryer in a home seemed like an afterthought. A dimly lit alcove in a hallway or a small, crowded space in a basement were typical "homes" for a laundry room. However, these days homeowners are demanding more space, storage, and a real room for doing the laundry. After all, each week you spend more time than you'd care to think about cleaning up the family wardrobe. Why not take some of the grunt out of the work by creating an efficient, well-equipped, and attractive place to get it done?

MAKING IT ATTRACTIVE

Just because you are doing laundry doesn't mean your surroundings should be bland and strictly utilitarian. Laminate faux-wood flooring is a great way to get the look of hardwood without the worry of moisture damage. Select neutral colors like taupe or honey for easy maintenance and to hide dirt. Another option is no-wax or resilient flooring or ceramic tile, which come in a wide range of colors. Or bring the outside in by installing exterior brick pavers on the floor. They are sturdy and easy to clean. No matter what flooring you use, soften the look and cushion your feet for standing and folding laundry with washable padded throw rugs.

BELOW Add personality with wallpaper and a fun motif. If the laundry is part of an extra bathroom, coordinate themes, colors, and materials. Sleek appliance design enhances decorative possibilities, as well.

OPPOSITE Cabinets on either side of the machine can store more than just laundry-related items. This is a good place to keep craft or hobby supplies or housekeeping items. A clean counter is a great place to fold clothes and linens.

FRONT-LOADING WASHERS: A LAUNDRY LIST OF BENEFITS

Once you would find front-loading washers only in a commercial laundromat. Now they are increasingly found in home laundry rooms. Here are some reasons:

■ Front-loading washers can be stacked with a dryer on top to conserve space. (See the photo, right.)

■ They spin clothes faster than a top-loading model, which is a more-efficient way of extracting water. This saves energy by requiring less time to dry a load of clothes in the dryer.

■ They use a wash process that is more gentle on clothing. In fact, some new machines have completely done away with an agitator.

■ They use less water, which lowers utility bills.

The one drawback of a front-loading model is that you can't pre-soak clothes as you can in a top-loading washer.

laundry and family rooms

MORE IDEAS

Color is the least expensive way to make a big impact while decorating your space. Semigloss paint and wallpaper are easy to clean and stand up well to any humidity. If you're family room will be open to the laundry area, use fabrics that are washable and can handle humidity. You might also consider dressing up your room with a custom faux painting on one wall or using a mirror on the wall opposite a window to fill your space with even more natural light.

When it comes to countertops, laminates are usually the surface of choice. Solid-surfacing material may be expensive, but in a family studio, it is a decorative advantage, especially is you like the faux stone versions. Laminates are durable, easy to clean up, and these days come in many patterns and colors. Other homeowners are taking a page from their kitchens and using ceramic-tile countertops Still others are combining a laundry room with a guest bath and tying both spaces together with custom-fabricated concrete or granite.

If you're planning a separate laundry, think about entertainment options to take the monotony out of the work before putting up walls. Wire a sound system into a laundry room so you can listen to your favorite music. Flush-mounted speakers installed in the ceiling are out of the way and inconspicuous. Include a table-top or wall-mounted TV.

LIGHTEN UP Typically, many homeowners don't give enough thought to lighting—and wind up regretting it. If you have the luxury of creating a laundry room near a basement window, do it. The natural

OPPOSITE If the room lacks natural light, paint the walls a bright color, add artwork and plants.

RIGHT A jetted sink spa is designed for delicates and eliminates the chore of washing by hand.

BELOW A standard kitchen sink is suitable for a laundry room, but pair it with a high-arched faucet.

BELOW RIGHT Plastic laminate is practical because it is impervious to water.

light will almost make you whistle while you work. Choose window treatments—whether they be shades, blinds, or curtains—that will allow light control and privacy at night. An overhead fixture will suffice in a small laundry room. But add task lighting to brighten work surfaces, accent any artwork in your space, and help you see what you're doing when treating clothing stains or sewing on a button. Consider installing under-cabinet or recessed lighting to illuminate work, or hang a pendant fixture over the folding table.

laundry and family rooms

ORGANIZE THE LAUNDRY AREA

Think about what you'll need for storage; then plan a place for everything, including laundry supplies, tools, hangers, mops, and brooms. Will your laundry room also double as pantry space or be a broom closet? As in kitchens and baths, a mixture of cabinets, shelves, and cubbies is the best way to go. Drawers are perfect for storing clothespins, sewing items, a toothbrush for scrubbing dirty tennis shoes. All laundry rooms need a space to hang clothing—a wooden dowel or a sturdy clothesline or a flat dryer rack for hand-washables. Install an extra counter space or a table just for folding clothes. Include a multi-compartment organizer to store homeless buttons or mate-less socks.

If space is at a premium, think about a fold-down ironing board that can be stored away when not in use or a folding arm for hanging clothes that can swivel out of your way. There are also miniature rolling laundry carts that can be neatly tucked away in a corner or between the washer and dryer.

There are an almost limitless number of options for upgrading a laundry room into a state-of-the-art laundry center. These days you can install drying cabinets that dry a wool sweater in a few hours or a clothes care valet system that removes wrinkles in 30 minutes.

If you're interested in combining your laundry facilities with a family room, remember that you can hide appliances behind handsome cabinet doors.

ABOVE Stackable machines conserve enough space to make room for an air-drying cabinet.

LEFT A no-frills laundry area can be tucked into a small kitchenette.

RIGHT Cabinetry can keep the ironing center out of view.

OPPOSITE A personal valet system is a new appliance that de-wrinkles and deodorizes clothes.

downstairs bedrooms

T hese days everyone expects a lot from a bedroom. It is a personal, private space, and a getaway from the pressures of daily living. For real comfort, there should be adequate storage space and furnishings that meet numerous needs, whether the space will be part of a master suite, a child's room, or a guest retreat. Whatever way you choose to decorate the room, make it attractive but soothing, providing the ultimate tranquility everyone needs at the end of the day. Here are some ideas for bedrooms, both basic and sublime.

LEFT **There is no one way to decorate a bedroom, except that it should be a very personal space.**

color and light

Sunlight, or the lack of it, has an effect on your mood. In a room that doesn't get much natural light, let color and artificial light banish the dark and uplift your spirits.

A WAY WITH COLOR The colors in a bedroom can enhance the atmosphere that you want to achieve. For instance, pinks and yellows will add to the sun's warm morning hues, while greens and blues have the reverse effect, making the room feel cool, fresh, and larger. Pure white can serve as the perfect backdrop for a colorful bedspread and window treatment.

For relaxing, soft colors will work best. You can choose any color in the rainbow, just keep it subtle. Reserve bright color hues for the wall behind the headboard. Complement it by painting a softer tone of the same color on the other three walls.

Don't forget the ceiling. After all, it is the first thing you'll see when you open your eyes in the morning. For a fresh approach, paint it a pale sky blue. It will make the room feel just a bit larger, and definitely airy. Or try your hand at a mural; apply crown molding where the ceiling meets the top of the wall; or stencil a design around the perimeter of the ceiling.

ABOVE A floral-pattern wallpaper looks fresh and springlike.

OPPOSITE TOP LEFT Pretty pastel colors have youthful appeal.

OPPOSITE TOP RIGHT Shutters are versatile on the window.

OPPOSITE A private retreat has direct access to the garden.

BRING IN THE GARDEN

I f your bedroom looks out on a beautifully landscaped yard or a terrace of potted plants, play up this bonus. If not, create your own bedroom "garden" with the decorating scheme. Here are a few easy to do ideas.

- Use an antique metal gate as a headboard. Secure it into the studs in the wall. Or use a section of a picket fence or garden trellis.
- Move a baker's rack into the bedroom, and use it to organize houseplants, accessories, and gardening books.
- Use picnic baskets at the foot of the bed for storage.
- Use floral patterns on the windows and the bedspread.
- Use watering cans as vases on a bureau or shelf, and arrange fresh-cut or dried flowers in them.

ABOVE Soft low-voltage halogens that are recessed into the soffit over this bed create a focal point in the room in addition to serving a useful purpose.

ENHANCING THE ROOM WITH LIGHT

Lighting, both natural and artificial, is important in creating a bedroom atmosphere. If the room receives lots of sunlight, you should provide a means for controlling it.

WINDOW TREATMENTS Covering the bedroom windows in layers is a good idea. This way, you have the option of full light, filtered light, or total blackout for sleeping in on lazy mornings. A sheer or thin blind will provide filtered light. A blackout-lined curtain will protect you from the morning sun. Decorate for the different seasons by backing heavier winter draperies with a floral pattern. Once spring has sprung, turn the rod around to reveal the lighter theme. Or use separate rods for heavy draperies and sheer curtains. Remove the draperies during the warm weather, leaving just the sheers in place with adjustable shades or blinds for light control.

LAMPS Use fixtures that will provide general lighting, but don't forget about lamps for reading or watching TV. Wall sconces can add soft illumination that's fine for viewing or relaxing, but task lighting is necessary for reading a book. Be careful with overhead spots that are aimed straight down on a book or paper. Although they leave nightstands free for books, glasses, clock-radio, and what-not, they might cast a shadow. Another option is to mount reading lights right on the headboard or to the side of the bed.

BASIC BED AND HEADBOARD STYLES

The style of bed you choose can quickly transform the room. Some have both a headboard and a footboard (below), while others may have just a headboard or a frame. Here are some different types.

- Sleigh beds. With a headboard and footboard that curve upward and resemble an old-fashioned sleigh, sleigh beds work well in rooms with low ceiling heights.
- Four-poster beds. The posts can have elaborate finials or decorative additions. When a canopy is attached, this is called a tester. Unlike the sleigh bed, four-posters only work well in bedrooms with high ceilings.
- Brass/iron beds. Some antique metal beds can be quite elaborate and provide an instant touch of charm to a bedroom. However, they are uncomfortable to use if you like to sit up and read in bed.
- Upholstered beds. An upholstered headboard and footboard are very comfortable if you sit in your bed to read and watch television.
- Trundle beds. Instead of a box spring supporting a mattress, the bed is made up of a mattress that is supported by a frame. Under this structure is housed another bed that be reached by simply pulling it out from underneath the main bed. Trundle beds provide additional sleeping space when needed.
- Platform beds. A mattress is placed on a wooden platform that provides the support for the sleeper. The platform can house various drawers, cupboards, and cabinets for clothing, linen, and accessory storage. The headboard is flanked with bookcases and built-in night tables. Platform beds are perfect when storage is at a premium.
- Murphy beds. Named for its designer, the Murphy bed folds up into an armoire, a wall unit, or even a closet when not in use.

thoughtful
storage

You can never have too much storage space. Closet systems, either designed from scratch and built by a closet organizing company or purchased in a store already assembled, can double the capacity of an ordinary space by maximizing it.

Closets typically have only one clothing rod with a lot of wasted space above and below it. Raise the existing rod, and add another one at waist level. Buy storage containers and shelves for shoes, handbags, and sweaters. Keep the clothing you wear most often where you can reach it easily.

STORAGE FURNITURE Invest in an armoire. Available in a range of styles and sizes, armoires usually have drawers for stowing sweaters and blankets, plus clothing rods for hanging shirts, jackets, and trousers. Add storage by buying nightstands with deep drawers and an upholstered ottoman with concealed storage beneath the seat.

MORE IDEAS Don't forget the area under the bed. Buy storage boxes, especially ones designed to fit under the box spring. Some are on wheels or glide on a track. These are great for linens or seasonal items.

Buy a folding screen. It not only makes for a neat room divider in the bedroom but can also hide clutter. Keep items in baskets and out of view.

SMART TIP

If you have a lot of built-in storage in the basement, you may not need a lot of other furniture in the room, which could provide the large space required for a luxurious king-size bed.

OPPOSITE TOP Use nightstands with deep drawers.

OPPOSITE BOTTOM Baskets can be hidden under a skirted bed-side table.

ABOVE Inexpensive plastic storage drawers look like furniture.

TOP RIGHT Built-ins enhance an adjacent dressing room.

RIGHT A four-poster bed will require a high ceiling, as well as a large room.

furnishings

Any bedroom benefits from a focal point, a single element that immediately draws attention and anchors the room with its visual weight or uniqueness. In the bedroom, the bed often plays this role. Four-posters, with and without canopies, are focal points because of their sheer height. A large or elaborate headboard can also do the trick. Even plain beds can be turned into attention grabbers if you dress them up with a dust ruffle, showy coverlet, and throw pillows on top. Other furniture can also serve as a focal point. It could be an antique blanket chest at the foot of the bed or a large table used as a desk.

When choosing other furniture, think in terms of proportion, selecting a piece that balances the weight of the bed. As a general rule, allow at least 36 to 40 inches in front of chests and dressers to pull out drawers. Choose chairs, trunk, and tables in keeping with the

SMART TIP

When lighting the bedroom with lamps, you should be able to see the lower edge of the shade when you are seated. If this edge is below your eye level, you are not getting enough illumination from the source. The average seating eye level is 38 to 42 inches above the floor.

ABOVE Accessorizing with wall art adds a finishing touch to the decor.

LEFT A computer desk and under-bed drawers outfit a compact room.

OPPOSITE Curtains suspended from a rod attached to the ceiling divide a space.

CRACKING THE CODES

Before you locate a bedroom in your remodeled basement, familiarize yourself with important building and safety codes. Here's what to keep in mind while you're making your plans.

- For safe exits in event of fire, all sleeping rooms above or below grade are required to have either a door to the outside or a window with 5.7 square feet of operable area through which a person can escape.
- Installation of a smoke detector in a sleeping room is required. Ironically, carbon monoxide detectors are not required by code.

scale of other pieces. Match the height of bedside tables to the bed, making sure the tables are at least as high as the top of the mattress. This will provide the best reading light from lamps set on the stands. Tuck a small bench at the foot of the bed or a diminutive chair in one corner to add seating options and provide space for books, clothes, or throws.

FLOORS Because people hop out of bed barefoot, it is always comforting to have a well-padded carpet underfoot. On the other hand, the earthiness of wood or a wood-laminate floor might be more appealing to you, and they are not as cold or hard as stone or concrete. You can soften and warm up these types of floors with area rugs. Carpet alternatives for anyone who has allergies can include vinyl, cork, ceramic tile, or stone, in addition to wood or a wood laminate.

OPPOSITE
Rooms that don't have a lot of clutter are easier to keep clean and free of dust mites.

BELOW Carpeting and uphostery can harbor allergens. Vacuum the room often and use bedding with antiallergen encasings.

RIGHT Washable curtains, rugs, blankets, quilts, pillow shams, and other bedding are recommended when allergies are a problem.

ALLERGY-FREE BEDROOMS

- In spring and summer, close the windows in the bedroom to keep allergens out.
- If you have plants in your bedroom, it's important to have a barrier between the plant and the carpet to prevent a problem with mold or mildew and water spillage.
- Painted walls are best for the bedroom because they are easy to clean. With wallpaper, you could have an allergic reaction to the paste.
- When selecting a lamp for the bedroom, stay away from the more-ornate designs because they can attract dust more easily than a simplistic design. Be sure to regularly clean and dust the lampshades.
- Hard floors — wood or stone — won't retain allergens the way rugs do. You should use carpeting only if you vacuum it frequently.
- Minimize the number of toss pillows on the bed. They collect a lot of dust and allergens.
- Ban your pet from the bed and, if you can manage it, the bedroom itself.
- Use wooden shutters or blinds on bedroom windows. Curtains and drapes harbor allergens and are more difficult to clean.

home office and workshop

Statistics indicate that two out of every ten adults regularly work out of the home and three out of ten do so on at least a part-time basis. A well-designed space will help improve not only your efficiency but also your overall work experience. When locating a home office or workshop in your newly redesigned basement, there is a laundry list of organizational and design issues that need to be addressed. Here's how to maximize the space and your time spent creating, whether it's a Power-Point presentation or a new bookshelf.

LEFT A finished basement is a perfect place for setting up an organized work space at home.

home office and workshop

a home office that really works

The first thing to consider is the type of worker you are. Do you need absolute privacy and quiet while slogging through a report, or does a little household hubbub in the background help you think creatively? Your answer will help determine the kind of home office or workshop you will need.

If you are the former, carve out space in a corner of the basement away from rooms that might be noisy—a laundry room or hobby room with video game consoles. You might also consider installing extra insulation in the walls and ceiling to further cut down on noise pollution. Sound-absorbing wall-to-wall industrial carpet and a heavy wood door with a lock might complete the picture.

If you are the latter type, however, you might design your office in a semi-open space with curvy glass block partial walls that won't completely close you off from the rest of the space. You may want to locate your office next to the family room or another hub where you family regularly comes together.

LEFT A compact spot is all you need for e-mailing or shopping on-line.

ILLUMINATING IDEAS

As with media rooms, light-colored walls or overdoing the use of mirrors in a basement home office will increase glare and possibly eyestrain. It's best to stick with warm neutrals or a color you like and wouldn't mind living with for a long period of time.

With window treatments, choose a type that can be adjusted to eliminate glare caused by the sun. Curtains with light-blocking insulated backs or wood blinds or shutters are attractive choices. If your space is window-less, create your own "sun" with full-spectrum light bulbs that simulate natural sunlight.

LIGHTING Proper lighting is important for anyone spending long hours working in an office environment. (For specific information on lighting, see Chapter 4, "Turn on the Light," page 42.)

IN GENERAL The best choices for diffuse illumination from all of the light sources in a room, artificial and natural, are a combination of table lamps and ceiling fixtures. Use dimmers to modify light levels to your changing needs. Low-voltage halogen bulbs or fluorescent bulbs will cut down on heat.

Good choices for task lighting include an adjustable fixture—preferably located behind your shoulder and to the side of the work surface—that can be directed where you need it. Add a table lamp. Another option is a light bridge that's built into the workstation itself.

TOP LEFT AND RIGHT If you need a full-time office for working at home, include amenities that will increase your comfort.

ABOVE Plan the lighting with care. Include overall general illumination, but don't forget task and accent lighting.

OUTFITTING THE OFFICE

As systems become integrated, with the monitor, computer, and the CD and DVD drives combined into one unit, office furniture is changing as well. Form is indeed following function. The new generation of worksta-

tions accommodates large monitors and provides room for peripherals such as a CD burner, scanner, additional hard drives, and so on. Some units contain ample storage for printer and fax paper, as well as envelopes, paper clips, pens and pencils, and staples.

Choose a unit with a locking mechanism for key-

RIGHT Paint the room your favorite color; add artwork and attractive, comfortable furniture.

OPPOSITE LEFT Locate the office away from the hub if you need quiet and privacy.

OPPOSITE RIGHT Keep your desktop neat to work more efficiently, especially in a room that serves more than one activity.

board trays that pull out for those times when you have to remind yourself to get down to business.

NEAT TRICKS Keep your work area uncluttered—just a computer, phone, and paper, pens, and pencils. Look for furniture with compartments. Workstations made of high-pressure laminates stand up to the daily abuse of opening and closing of drawers and compartments; wood to a lesser degree, especially if the space retains some moisture. If occasional dampness is a problem, use a dehumidifier. It will also speed up the drying time of documents printed on ink-jet printers.

SMART TIP

Think vertical when planning for storage. A floor-to-ceiling bookshelf, with doors or drawers at its base, is the most efficient configuration and doesn't gobble up valuable floor space in the process. Store items that you don't regularly need handy on the top shelves.

THE ABC'S OF OFFICE LAYOUT

With a home office, efficiency of usage should always take precedence over appearance. Decorative aspects can then be adapted to work within the confines of the most useful arrangement. Here are three common home office configurations:

- Parallel. Extra work surfaces, such as a credenza to hold a fax machine or copier, can be placed either behind or in front of the main work desk.
- L-shape. A secondary work surface is attached at a right angle to the main desk. This is especially useful when standard pen-and-paper deskwork is combined with the use of a personal computer.
- U-shape. A variation on the L-shape, this configuration features two secondary work surfaces at right angles to the main work area. U-shape layouts have the same advantages, as the L-shape arrangement, only more.

STORAGE This is a must for any home office. The rule of thumb is that everything important to doing the job should be within comfortable arm's reach, which leaves quite a bit that needs to be stored away. Custom cabinets are the most efficient, using every available square inch of space. Or use a freestanding, pre-assembled closet organizer for supplies and files or adapt stock kitchen cabinetry with rollout drawers, lazy Susans, and other space-saving features to your office needs. Get creative. Hang files in an old trunk, or store office supplies in clear plastic stacking cubes or modules.

WIRING It's a smart idea to add an extra circuit to isolate your computer and other office equipment from power to the rest of your house. Drawing too much power from one circuit can trip circuit breakers and cause the loss of valuable information. Allow enough electrical circuits and install an extra phone line or two in case you have to move equipment around if you rearrange the room.

When shopping for a computer table or unit, look for models that provide large grommets for those extra yards of annoying wires. Cord control is extremely important to the aesthetics of your home office and to your safety. Home-computer users have been known to trip over the odd cable, knocking over their monitor in the process. A wide range of cable organizers and holders, some of them quite ingenious, are available in computer stores. To minimize a tangle of cords and cables on the floor, you can also have an outlet or phone jack installed on top of your computer desk or mounted on the side of a base cabinet.

PAIN-FREE COMPUTING

Camping out in front of a computer can be a pain in the neck, wrist, eyes, hips, ankles...you get the picture. Here are some tips to take the ouch out of prolonged stints at the computer.

- Buy an adjustable chair (arm rests, seat pan, height) with a five-wheel base. The front of the chair should tip or tilt forward slightly to give you proper legroom. At a minimum, the chair should be curved at the front so as not to cut off the circulation in your legs.
- You should be about an arm's length away from the monitor screen when you're sitting back in the chair. Your eyes should be level with an imaginary line that is about 2 or 3 inches below the top of the monitor.
- When word processing, keep your wrists in a neutral (straight) position and your elbows at a 90-degree or greater angle. Use a light touch when typing (don't bang the keys), and don't use wrist rests and armrests when you're typing, only when resting.
- If you work for prolonged periods at a time, follow the 20-20-20 rule. Take a 20-second break every 20 minutes and look at least 20 feet away to give your eyes a rest and a change of focus. After 30 minutes, get up and move around and do some light stretching.

SMART TIP

Using a low-pile industrial carpet instead of a plusher weave will smooth the transition of your computer chair and other portable equipment from one part of the room to the next.

BELOW Home-office furniture that is open underneath keeps the look light.

RIGHT AND RIGHT BOTTOM A desktop organizer keeps supplies neat and handy. Protect important files in a cabinet or a plastic file keeper.

workshops and studios down under

Basements make ideal locations for exploring a creative passion, whether that be woodworking or crafting. Away from the buzz of household activity, you can hear yourself think and, when you're ready to create, all of your tools and materials are at your fingertips—if you plan the space properly.

For most workshops, a triangle layout works best, with the main focal points of your hobby or craft located at the three corners. In a shop geared toward woodworking, for example, wood and lumber storage, along with larger power tools like a table saw and jointer, is positioned at one corner of the triangle. A workbench is placed at the second corner, which is usually in the center of the room. Here you would use hand tools or smaller power tools such as a hand drill, router, or joining tool. The finishing station is located at the third corner, where the fine, detailed work takes place. The triangle also works well for a sewing or craft studio.

Here are some tips to help you create a workshop that is attractive, efficient, and safe.

LIGHTING THE WORKSHOP

Adequate lighting is critical in this setting. Think about your general lighting needs first, then about requirements for specific areas of the workshop.

OVERHEAD LIGHTING Fluorescent fixtures are usually a good choice for overhead lighting. They are inexpensive, easy to install, and energy efficient, and they put out a lot of light. They cast an even light over the entire workshop. Wire overhead lights so that they are on a separate circuit from the wall outlets. That way, if a power overload from a tool trips a circuit breaker, the lights will remain on.

TRACK LIGHTING Track lighting is another good choice for overhead illumination and is best suited for focusing on a particular spot in the workshop. Flood bulbs can be used to light larger areas, while spot bulbs can focus concentrated light on smaller spaces. An advantage with track lights is that individual lights can be redirected into different places should you decide to rearrange your workshop.

UNDER-CABINET LIGHTING Halogen or fluorescent strips can be installed underneath shelves and cabinet bottoms to illuminate very specific areas of the work sur-

FAN FACTS

The easiest way to ventilate your workshop is with a fan. These come in a large array of styles and sizes:

- Industrial fans can move large amounts of air and are good for a large shop.
- Oscillating fans move back and forth to enhance circulation. These won't get rid of chemical fumes, just blow them around.
- Exhaust fans move fumes and stale air out of the workshop to the outside.
- Box fans, inexpensive and portable, can be set up in a window to bring in outside air or turned around to draw out stale air.
- Enclosed fans, teamed up with air filters, can be installed in ductwork to suck out dirty air and return filtered air into the workspace.

face. This type of lighting is ideal in small places where detailed work is done.

PORTABLE LAMPS Portable floodlights are handy for specific jobs. Directional, height-adjustable, and bright, they're ideal for focusing light in awkward places.

SMART TIP

Apply an epoxy paint to a basement's concrete floor for a tough, durable surface. Stir sand into the paint to prevent slips if the floor gets wet or slick. Or install sheet vinyl, which provides some cushioning under your feet and is easy to clean.

ABOVE Store hazardous materials inside a locked cabinet.

RIGHT A pegboard rack keeps clutter off the work bench.

LEFT A roll-away tool-cart can move around the shop with you. Supplement it with a portable tool box.

BELOW LEFT Keep a portable light handy for illuminating tight corners or awkward spaces, such as under the attic eaves.

BELOW RIGHT Free up floor space—and avoid tripping—by installing a wall rack for the ladder.

RIGHT Power tools and hand tools can be stored on special wall racks to keep them out of the way, but easy to locate.

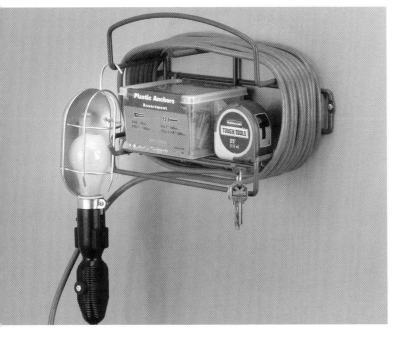

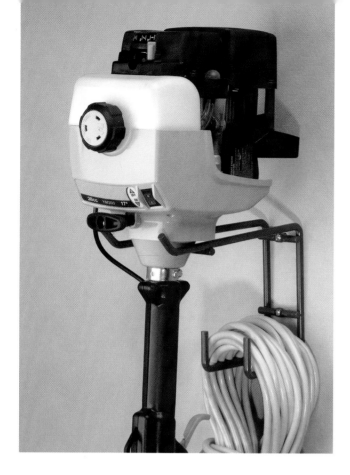

ORGANIZING THE WORKSHOP

Most experts recommend two operable windows in a workshop as well as one or two fans. (See "Fan Facts," on page 110.) Woodworking shops produce a lot of dust. Install a dust-collection system to keep it under control. Without one, dust will find its way into forced-air heating and cooling systems and settle throughout the house. Have vacuum hoses connected to every power tool. Also install weatherstripping on doors for dust and noise control, not to mention extra insulation in the first-story floor joists to keep shop noises from disturbing the rest of the house.

Well-planned storage can help you keep your work-shop organized and, equally important, free up countertop and workbench space. Small additions can make a big difference. A simple feature like a rubber drawer liner in a storage cabinet, for example, can prevent tools from sliding around and becoming disheveled when the drawers are opened and closed.

CABINETS Plan a combination of stationary and mobile cabinets on casters, which can be moved around the shop as necessary and stored underneath a workbench when not in use. Many mobile and stationary cabinets contain pullout shelves that make it easy to see and reach tools at both the front and rear of each shelf. Tall storage cabinets are ideal for storing larger power hand tools and similar items.

Some cabinets are designed to be hung on the wall. A slat-wall system uses composite panels that are simply fastened to the walls. The composite panels are easy to install and are designed to withstand heat, cold, and humidity. Once the weight-bearing wall panels are in place, modular cabinets can be easily hung by placing the pre-attached hooks into the slat and locking them into place. The panels can also accommodate other items such as baskets, shelves, and even some tools.

SHELVES Adjustable wall-mounted shelving is a staple for workshops. You can remove and reposition the brackets to adjust the height of the shelves to suit your changing needs. Floor-standing shelves can also handle some of the storage load.

SAFETY FIRST

One of the most important things to plan for in a workshop is safety. Here are some suggestions.

■ Keep a first-aid kit in your workshop, and always know where it is.

■ Wear plastic goggles or safety glasses when using any power tools. Leave the goggles in a hard-to-miss location—such as on the table of a drill press—as a reminder to wear them.

■ Use full-sized ear-muff-style ear protection or at least ear plugs when using high-decibel power tools such as table saws and circular saws.

■ Wear protective respirators or dust masks to avoid breathing dust and other particulate pollutants.

■ Install a smoke detector and a fire extinguisher in the workshop.

■ Locate your circuit breaker box where it's easily accessible.

■ Install a phone, which is an essential piece of equipment in case of emergencies.

home gyms and spas

A carefully planned, well-appointed at-home spa or gym is an increasingly popular choice when redesigning a basement. Dedicating a modest-sized space for a gym is a wise investment. Studies show that you will exercise more regularly when you have the room and a wide range of equipment at your fingertips. A 10 x 12-foot space with 7- or 8-foot-high ceilings can accommodate two pieces of cardio equipment, a weight bench, and dumbbells. Plus, setting up a spa or gym is often easier and costs less than you may think.

LEFT **Create your own at-home retreat, complete with all of the amenities of an upscale spa.**

gyms: exercise your options

The best bonus from putting an exercise room in your basement is not the money you will save on gym memberships or the time you save on trips to the health club. Rather, it's that you'll find time to work out. For some reason, people who put in a gym, as opposed to a treadmill in the bedroom, tend to actually use it.

Here are some no-sweat design considerations when setting up a home gym.

CREATE A COMFORT ZONE

Concrete slab floors found in most basements are a blessing and a curse. They can support the heavy work-out machines, but they are hard to stand on for long periods of time. Whatever you put down should be able to take a lot of wear and tear. Vinyl or rubber tiles at least ⅜-inch thick are a practical and inexpensive option: they offer more protection and cushion than carpeting and are maintenance free. (A few swipes of a damp rag will clean them.)

ABOVE LEFT Incorporate a bath and dressing room.

LEFT Low-pile carpeting is one way to soften a concrete floor.

RIGHT Hardwood can be fine in a home gym, especially for aerobic workouts.

SMART TIP

When planning space for a home gym, factor in room between the machines to prevent banging your arms and legs during a workout. Experts agree that there should be a minimum of 30 inches between pieces of exercise equipment.

VENTILATION AND LIGHT Planning your gym in a section of the basement that has several operable windows serves two purposes: looking outside takes your mind off of the workout and opening a window allows you to get fresh air in a room that can quickly get stuffy and stale. Window treatments such as wooden shutters or miniblinds will allow you to screen out the sun during the hot summer months. If windows aren't an option, arrange electrical outlets to include a large overhead fan. Standing oscillating fans can also take the heat off when doing a tough workout.

Track-mounted or recessed fixtures can direct supplemental lighting where it's needed without getting in your way as you exercise.

Neutrals and warm whites on the walls will make the gym feel brighter and more spacious, both of which can enhance motivation. Lightweight, shatter-proof acrylic mirror panels on the walls will also reflect natural and ambient light and enable you to check out your form while strength-training.

WIRING If you are a dedicated aerobic dancer, then make sure to upgrade and arrange wiring, cable, and receptacles so that you can easily use a TV and a DVD player or VCR. Many people like a little entertainment to take the boredom out of their exercise routine, too. Integrate wiring from your media room into your gym layout, so you can listen to music while working out. Flush-mounted speakers in the ceiling or speakers mounted in the four corners of the room provide rich sound without getting in the way of your gym equipment. If you spend a lot of time on the treadmill, fixing a TV on a swiveling, ceiling-mounted corner bracket allows you to view the set from anywhere in the room.

GYM EQUIPMENT

To accommodate your cardiovascular and strength-training needs, you will probably want one or two cardio machines and either a set of dumbbells or a weight-lifting station. A stationary bike remains an evergreen among home gym enthusiasts because it takes up little space and can be used by those who suffer from knee, hip, lower back, or weight problems. Elliptical trainers and treadmills are the most popular cardio machines. Treadmills are perhaps the most versatile, allowing you to either walk or run on them. To prevent workout boredom, it is wise to have more than one machine.

In terms of strength training, you have two options: free weights (dumbbells and a bar and metal weights) or an all-in-one weight-lifting station with a bench. If you will be working out alone most of the time, the latter is probably the best choice because you don't have to worry about being crushed under the bar if the weight is too heavy.

home gyms and spas

spas that
pamper

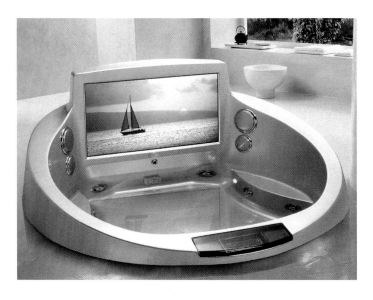

Home spas generally are designed in combination with home gyms because there is nothing more relaxing to muscles than a stint in a steam shower or sauna after a taxing workout.

The basement is an ideal space to add a home spa because plumbing and electrical service are centrally located and easily accessible there. In addition, the concrete-slab floor can support a hot tub filled with water or some of the new heavy whirlpool bathtubs without any structural reinforcement.

FEEL-GOOD FEATURES

When you visit a commercial spa, it's the employees who pamper you with massages and wraps. In your home spa, a new generation of tubs and showers outfitted with specialty fixtures do the job. Do you want to be calmed or invigorated? Or both? There is a bathtub for you.

WHIRLPOOLS A typical upgrade is a whirlpool tub with jets that force out air to create a massaging effect. Many tubs offer jets that can be redirected to massage a sore neck or back or adjusted to increase or decrease pressure. One downside: you can't use bath oils or salts, which can cause bacterial growth inside the jet tubes.

AIR JETS You can use aromatic oils in tubs with air systems. This

ABOVE Soothe your tired limbs and sore muscles while you watch a movie.

BELOW A soaking tub is extra deep so that you can submerge your body, but it doesn't take up a lot of floor space.

OPPOSITE Lean back and relax while you enjoy a relaxing massage or invigorating muscle therapy in a multi-jetted tub.

type has 30 to 70 small holes drilled around the radius of the tub that emit soft, gentle bubbles. Some air-system tubs are also equipped with whirlpool jets.

SOAKING TUBS Soaking tubs are deeper than but not as long as standard tubs. They allow you to submerge yourself comfortably in water up to your neck.

EXTRAS For a bathing experience, look for special features, such as air and water jets that can simulate the sensation of river rapids. Some showerheads produce a "rain shower" while some spouts deliver a "waterfall."

ABOVE **A peaceful Zen-like aesthetic can be achieved by keeping the environment simple.**

LEFT **A prefabricated shower can come with multiple adjustable showerheads.**

OPPOSITE **Customize the experience with a shower tower.**

SPLENDOR IN THE SHOWER

If you don't have the time to wait for an oversize tub to fill up, think about spa showers. Today's showerheads and sprays offer the massaging action of whirlpool jets without the wait. A shower is almost always separate from the tub, although it's common to see the tub deck extend into the shower compartment to serve as a bench or a ledge for shampoo, for example.

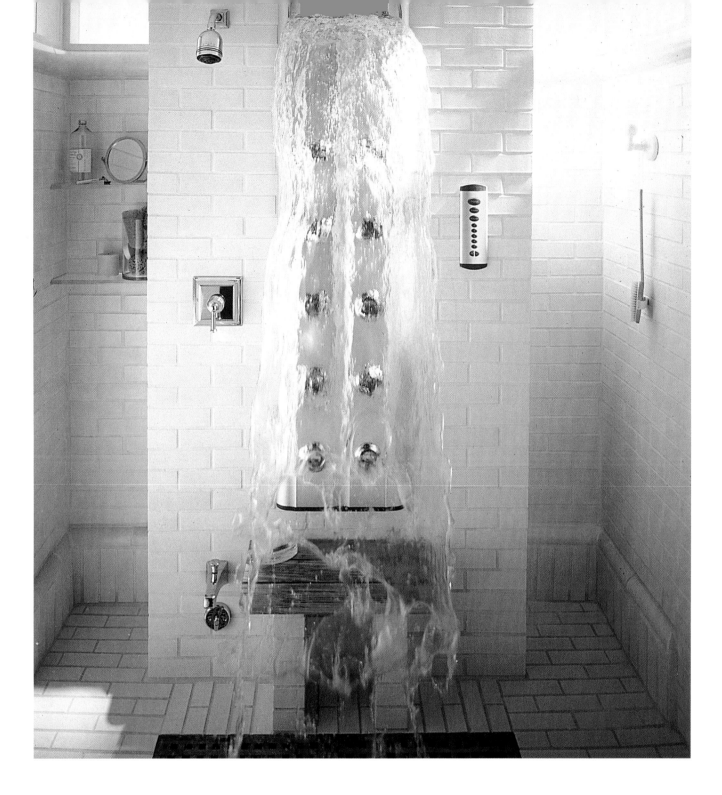

WATER DELIVERY Some showerheads are positioned to hit the body first in case you don't want to get your hair wet. For a whole-body shower, try a rain dome—a wide-diameter head mounted on the ceiling—that emits a large volume of water but a gentle flow. Or consider a shower tower: four to ten jets are positioned in a vertical column to reach every part of the body. Don't forget to equip your shower with a thermostatic valve, which allows you to preset the temperature.

STEAM FEATURES Steam showers have become extremely popular. A steam generator is built right into the shower stall, which is tightly enclosed from the ceiling to the floor. You can include an oversized bench in the design and a whirlpool foot bath that can be recessed into the shower stall's floor.

If this isn't enough pampering, you might want to consider one or two other features for your home health club.

home gyms and spas

SAUNAS AND HOT TUBS

Who hasn't headed to a sauna after an agonizing workout on the ellliptical trainer or treadmill? It is a luxury many have thought about having in their own home. Installing one in your basement is easier than you think. Because they use dry heat, saunas don't require a water supply or drain. What's more, the sauna stove can be tied directly into existing household circuits.

The original Finnish sauna was a one-room log cabin heated with a woodstove. Today, there are multiple options limited only by the amount of space you have and your budget. Some saunas even incorporate softly lit dressing rooms, massage rooms, and cold-water plunges.

Prefab units, both compact and grand, come with doors, paneled walls, sauna stove, and all hardware. Larger versions include a bar and bedroom. Some saunas are made of cedar and provide a soothing fragrance when heated up. Infrared saunas heat the body directly rather than circulating hot air throughout the enclosure.

Any time you install a sauna, include ventilation to take care of any condensation that might build up on the outside of the sauna as well as extra insulation in the walls to provide energy efficiency.

HOT TUBS Today's hot tub has a lining that is made of acrylic, thermoplastic, or soft vinyl, and its shell may come in a wide spectrum of colors and textures including a faux granite. A typical unit is 5 to 6 feet in diameter and has a depth of 3 to 4 feet.

Always wet-test a hot tub in the showroom to make sure it's comfortable and that the jets direct water where you want it. Some of the newer models have integrated aroma-therapy systems, stereo systems with waterproof speakers, built-in TVs, and LED underwater lights that change color. Also, make sure that you can reach the controls without leaving the water.

ABOVE The ideal sauna room is about 7 feet high. People sitting on the upper bench will enjoy maximum heat of about 165 to 195 degrees Fahrenheit with a minimum amount of preset time.

ABOVE RIGHT A sauna can be enjoyed alone or with others. In this large lighted sauna, it can be a social place to share with friends. Because the temperature is highest near the ceiling, children and the elderly should use the lower benches.

RIGHT Spa manufacturers often let you customize your bathing experience with a host of pampering options.

setting
the mood

Natural light spilling through a window creates a relaxing backdrop for any spa. If access to daylight is a problem, borrow light from an adjoining area by creating a wall of sandblasted glass or glass block to allow light to pass through from another room without compromising privacy. Artificial light from ambient sources can add just the right atmosphere to your spa. Recessed fixtures can unobstrusively highlight design features and produce soft pools of light. Fixtures placed on either side of the vanity rather than on top, will shine a flattering glow on the face without shadows. Dimmer switches on all lights enable you to control the amount of illumination in the room by function and by area: brighter for dressing, softer for bathing. And don't overlook candlelight as a source of illumination. From pillar to votive candles, these highly portable and, in some cases, fragrant light sources can create the perfect ambiance for quiet meditation or a soothing bath.

RELAXED STYLE

Gracing your space with speakers that pipe in music from the media room will pamper your ears as well as

SAUNA ETIQUETTE AND SAFETY

- Remove jewelry, eyeglasses, and contact lenses. They may conduct heat in the sauna and become burning hot.
- Don't enter on a full stomach. Allow a couple of hours between the sauna and meals.
- Plan your time. Some people like to sauna after exercise to soothe sore muscles. Others prefer to sauna at the end of the day to bring on sleep.
- Vary the heat and length of stay. Novices need to build up endurance. Children, for example, should stick their feet in a bucket of cool water to moderate the impact of the heat.

OPPOSITE A heated towel rack can be installed on the floor or wall and comes in a choice of finishes.

ABOVE If space is tight, you can reserve a small area for a prefabricated shower unit.

RIGHT Enhance your experience by setting a relaxing mood after a high-energy workout.

your soul. Colors that gravitate toward gentle earth and water hues are ideal for home spas. Subtle blues, greens, and warm sand tones complete a serene and tranquil setting. Consider a small fountain, plants, or a garden statue to replicate the look and feel of the outdoors.

EXTRAS Use ornamental hooks throughout the spa area to keep robes within arm's reach. Store a generous supply of plush, oversized bath towels in a large basket next to the tub, shower, or exercise area. Install cabinets to house lotions, bath oils, and salts, along with hair dryers, curling wands, or any other personal grooming appliance you might use. A nearby mini-fridge can store an ample supply of mineral water or other refreshing beverages.

Electric heated towel bars and floor warmers installed underneath a stone or marble floor are wise additions when the weather turns cold. For added warmth, cozy up to a gas fireplace. There are two-way fireplaces that can face toward the spa and another room in your basement at the same time.

kitchens and baths

A kitchen is a convenience in a new basement space; a bathroom is a must. The kitchen, whether upstairs or downstairs, is the hub of any home. Even though you might have included a family room and second kitchen in your basement design, don't be surprised if people congregate in the kitchen area. As for a bathroom, you can liken it to a car. Compact models squeeze the basics into an economical package while large versions emphasize luxury. The thing to remember is that baths of all sizes can be functional and stylish.

LEFT The kitchen is probably the most-popular room in the house, even when it's located in the basement.

kitchen ideas

Whether you are creating a second full-time kitchen or a less ambitious kitchenette to conveniently handle those inevitable hunger pains or the kids' parties, there are lots of ways to make the space both functional and beautiful. Before getting started, check with your local building department to make sure that adding a second kitchen to your house is legal. If it is, here are some design ideas to help you with the planning.

CABINETS AND APPLIANCES

Cabinets and appliances are the two big-ticket items. When you think about it, cabinets are the real furniture of the kitchen. As a result, they should not only make a design statement but function well in the space. You can cut down on expenses without sacrificing good looks by buying stock cabinets and customizing them. You can actually find kits with precut ornamental pieces and self-adhesive backing.

CABINET CHOICES Cabinets made of plastic laminate—a thick particleboard underneath a laminate facing—come in a wide range of colors and patterns. Some of the newer speckled and patterned designs not only look great, but won't show minor scratches and scars. What's more, plastic-laminate cabinets can be refaced relatively inexpensively.

Wood cabinets offer the greatest variety of style and finish. Framed cabinets—the full frame spans the face of the cabinet and may show between the doors—are popular for achieving a traditional look. Problem is, they are slightly less roomy than frameless cabinets, which have full overlay doors and drawer fronts. If space is at a premium, go for the frameless type.

LEFT An under-cabinet microwave oven with a built-in exhaust fan and a ceramic cooktop are smart space-saving ideas for a kitchen anywhere in the house.

BELOW Stainless-steel appliances are popular for their sleek contemporary appearance. In this kitchen, the homeowner paired them with wood cabinets to achieve a modern yet warm look.

RIGHT White is always a classic choice. It makes any space feel larger. When you're shopping for cabinets, keep in mind how much storage you need, and look for options and accessories.

COMFORT AND SAFETY ARE IN THE DETAILS

The National Kitchen and Bath Association recommends the following tips when designing your kitchen:

- Choose flooring that is slip-resistant.
- Make sure any glass in cabinet doors is tempered.
- Keep a fire extinguisher handy.
- Provide ground-fault-circuit-interrupter (GFCI) protection for all electrical outlets.
- Install faucets with antiscald devices.
- Use clipped or radius corners and curved or beveled edges on countertops.
- Use proper lighting. Never work in a dim area.
- Choose a cooktop or stove with front or side controls. If you have to reach over a hot pot or burner to use a control, you can be scalded.
- Locate the microwave at a height that does not require reaching over your head.

NOW YOU'RE COOKIN' Choosing the right appliance is among the most important decisions you will make in your new kitchen. The choices in ovens and cooktops have grown exponentially in recent years. In addition to the standard four-burner model, there are commercial-style ranges that offer more precise heat control and six or more burners, which are especially good for homeowners who frequently entertain. Some models come with one continuous grate or sealed burners, so pots slide smoothly across the cooking surface. A popular option is having a separate cooktop and oven. Convection ovens cook faster than conventional ovens and slower than microwaves. New oven technology combines the benefits of both microwave and convection cooking within a single unit.

VENTILATION Where there is heat, there is smoke, so always include proper venitlation in your basement kitchen design plans. Hooded systems vented to the outside provide the most effective ventilation, removing smoky, greasy, smelly air that could ruin your surfaces or leave a stale cooking odor in the room. Hoods can be wall-mounted, cantilevered over a range, or installed above islands or peninsulas.

Many new ranges are self-ventilating and come equipped with a downdraft system that forces greasy air through a filter and then moves it through ductwork to the outside.

JUST CHILLIN' Even if you don't need another full-size kitchen, you should think about an extra refrigerator,

FAR LEFT The only way to combat the grease and grime that is generated by cooking is with an exhaust system. A range hood is usually quite effective.

LEFT TOP Some of the features of commercial equipment, such as high-heat and low-simmer burners, are offered in today's ranges.

LEFT BOTTOM A pair of wall ovens, even in a second kitchen, makes sense for homeowners who enjoy doing a lot of entertaining.

LEFT Compact state-of-the-art refrigeration can be concealed behind custom-cabinet doors.

ABOVE A drawer-size dishwasher fits neatly into a small space. Use it alone or in combination with a large model.

RIGHT A wine cooler lets you keep the right wine on hand at all times and chilled to the optimal temperature.

especially if your basement remodeling plans include a family or game room. Refrigerators come in all sizes and configurations. (See "The Big Chill: Fridge Facts," right.) For those who don't want a refrigerator intruding into the room or interrupting the line of cabinetry, choose a slim-line model that is not as deep as the standard types. Additional options include a modular freezer or refrigerator drawer that can be installed into a bank of cabinets, an island, or a peninsula, and even inside a small chest of drawers. These compact appliances can put refrigerated or frozen foods or soft drinks exactly where you need them, and they're convenient for kids to use.

THE DISH ON DISHWASHERS There's nothing worse than buying an expensive dishwasher only to find out that you can't fit oversized wine glasses, platters, or bowls in it. Bring some of your everyday and special dishes to the appliance store, and put them in the dishwasher before buying it. Dishwashers also come with a variety of extra features these days. Options include convection drying, concealed controls, built-in water softener, and modular drawer-size units. Noise is another important consideration, especially if the kitchen is located next to a media room or home office. Ask about noise levels before committing to a model. Many new models are whisper-quiet.

THE BIG CHILL: FRIDGE FACTS

Cubic feet can be a confusing concept when trying to figure out cold-storage needs. As a rule, start with 12 cubic feet of total refrigerator/freezer space for the first two family members. Add 2 cubic feet for each additional person who lives in your home.

There are three types of refrigerator available:

■ A top-mount refrigerator consists of a separate freezer compartment over the main storage food space. It's the most efficient refrigerator to operate and puts freezer items at a convenient height.

■ A bottom-mount model has the freezer compartment near the floor. The setup puts the most frequently used refrigerator space at a more accessible height. Some freezers pull out like a drawer, which is especially handy for a seated cook.

■ A side-by-side refrigerator and freezer design requires less space for opening the doors, which makes it a good fit for narrow galley kitchens where you want to keep the traffic area clear. Although a side-by-side freezer compartment offers more cubic feet of storage at more convenient levels, the unit's shelves and door are sometimes too small to hold large containers and bulky items.

kitchens and baths

SINKS AND FAUCETS

What could be more basic to a kitchen than a sink and faucet? But in today's world, there is nothing basic about them. Even if your basement kitchen will be modest and utilitarian, check out the array of choices that are available even in the modest price range of products. A sink made of stainless steel, enameled cast iron, or a composite material (solid-surfacing acrylic, for example) will serve you well. But the old-fashioned exposed-apron sink that would have been thought of as déclassé not too long ago is now a decorator item. If you have an old porcelain one in your basement, you might want to consider refinishing it and working it into your plans.

Be sure to match up your sink with a good-looking, serviceable faucet. Again, you can find lots from which to choose, but a sleek single-lever pullout faucet with a sprayer is practical. High-arc spouts make a lot of sense if the sink basin is shallow. For a few extra dollars, you can buy a faucet with a built-in water purifier to improve taste if necessary.

LEFT Stainless steel and solid-surfacing material look sleek and modern in this kitchen. Reproduction styling adds grace to the single-lever faucet.

BELOW As long as you seal wood against water, you can use it on the countertop. However, you will have to regularly maintain the finish to keep it watertight.

SURFACES

Depending upon how lavish you plan to make your basement kitchen, your choices in countertop material run the gamut.

Practical, affordable plastic laminate comes in various grades, colors, and patterns. The cheaper it is, the more likely it will chip, however. Solid-surfacing material, another synthetic material, is extremely durable, but it's expensive. Because the color goes through the entire thickness of the slab, it can be carved and shaped in many ways.

Tile is always attractive, but it requires periodic regrouting. Stone is top of the line. You may want to consider a handsome granite surface if you're doing custom work, in a bar or wine cellar where you will entertain, for example. Another material to consider is concrete, which can be poured into a custom mold, colored, shaped, carved, or inlaid with objects, such as pieces of stone or glass. Remember, concrete has to be sealed against water, and it can crack.

FLOORING Your kitchen floor, besides being practical and durable, is a major design statement. Stone or tile is an excellent choice for heavily trafficked areas. Ceramic tiles that closely mimic natural stones are now on the market. They have the advantage of being less expensive than the real thing and easier to maintain. Ceramic is reliable and available in assorted colors and styles with the option for decorative borders and designs. Cork is also durable and versatile, as well as being water-resistant. It is also quieter than most flooring. Today's prefinished wood floors withstand heavy traffic and water stains. High-pressure laminates are an alternative that provide the same look for less money.

SMART TIP

To allow flexibility in a kitchen's layout, consider having a separate oven and cooktop rather than a range, which combines both of these appliances.

ABOVE A family kitchen can be planned with several activity zones. Cabinet doors and appliances should not block walkways.

BELOW In a kitchen that's designed for gourmet cooks, equipment includes a professional range and refrigerator.

the road to a better bathroom

When designing a new downstairs bath, keep a couple of things in mind: building codes require 84 inches of headroom. A toilet and a shower will require either tying into an existing drain line or installling new plumbing and a new drain. Once the logistics have been settled, there is a wide range of design possibilities and product options from which to choose.

Many homeowners look at the basement as a logical place to add a powder room or an extra half bath. In the case of a powder room, you won't have to contend with the problems that are caused by steam and excessive moisture. However, a full-size bathroom is another story.

SMART TIP

To visually lower a very high ceiling in a bathroom, paint it a color that is several shades darker than that on the walls or use a heavily patterned wall-covering on it.

RIGHT Slate tiles are an excellent choice in a bathroom that will be equipped with a hot-steam shower.

BELOW Side lighting and a large mirror over the vanity are important for grooming tasks. A separate toilet room is useful in a shared bath.

PRACTICAL AND STYLISH

Ceramic tile has always been the material of choice in a bathroom because it is impervious to water and offers so many design possibilities. On the other hand, natural stone, particularly granite, has nudged out tile in popularity in recent years. Not only is it rich-looking, it is durable. But it's expensive, so you might want to consider a stone lookalike fabricated from solid-surfacing material or another laminate. Another cost-cutting alternative is stone tile, as opposed to slab stone. However, the latter offers design flexibility.

OTHER SURFACING OPTIONS Hardwood is eye-pleasing, but it will require regular upkeep in a high-humidity bathroom. Wall-to-wall carpet and moisture aren't a good marriage either. Consider using washable throw rugs (with nonskid backing), instead, to add color, texture, or a pattern on the floor. Resilient vinyl flooring is a low-cost option that will last at least 20 years and resists mold and mildew.

PAINT When you're choosing paint for the walls, look for one that contains a mildewcide. Eggshell, satin, or semigloss resists moisture better than flat paints. Wallpaper is another option. Use moisture-resistant, scrubbable vinyl wallpaper for the best results.

FIXTURES

A trend these days is to compartmentalize various areas within the bathroom. The so-called toilet room, in which the toilet is contained on its own or partially enclosed by a knee wall or a half wall, is an example. While a separate toilet compartment is great for privacy it requires the space. If the basement bathroom will be shared by two or more people, it might be a good idea to plan individual zones for grooming, toileting, showering, and bathing.

TOILETS There are two styles of toilets: standard and elongated bowls. Two inches longer than the standard models, elongated toilets are considered more comfortable and sanitary. Sleek one-piece models fit into contemporary decor while traditional two-piece models (a tank and a bowl) come in a range—from Mediterranean to Victorian.

TUBS A relaxing bath doesn't require a sumptuous tub. A standard 60-inch-long model will do. A roomy soaking tub, which usually comes 42 inches wide, certainly has its advantages, though. You can find models these days with a built-in head rest at one end and other convenient options, including drink holders. Because most basement floors are concrete, why not look into a vintage cast-iron tub with lion's-claw feet. Beyond the typical porcelain, enameled-over cast iron, fiberglass, and acrylic versions, tubs can be made of everything from concrete and mosaic tile to marble, stone, and even wood.

Whirlpool tubs add convenience and comfort while increasing the resale value of your house. Whirlpools come in all shapes and colors. Some are outfitted with jets that pump water and air at variable speeds. Multiple-jetted tubs can massage your feet or your shoulders.

SHOWERS Showers have become the new status symbol in luxury bathrooms. Like whirlpool tubs, showers can now be outfilled with steam, multiple message jets, or even video and audio equipment. A shower can be designed to be separate from the tub or to take the place of the tub altogether. If you don't like to take a lot of long baths, this makes sense.

SMART TIP

Proper ventilation should be part of any bathroom design. Bathroom fans usher damaging moisture and odors to the outside. Look for an exhaust fan that can move a lot of air (measured in cubic feet per minute, or cfm) without making a lot of noise (measured in sones). Fans can range from 1 sone (the quietest) to more than 4 sones. Some units come complete with infrared heating and lighting fixtures. Make sure to put the fan on a separate switch from the lights to avoid hearing it roar (unless it's a quiet model) every time you flick the switch. Fresh air is important. Combining a fan with an operable window will maximize ventilation.

SINKS In small spaces, pedestal sinks are a good choice. Handsome yet compact, they add elegance to a plain bathroom. The only downside? You lose storage space. This may not be a big deal if there is a linen closet in or near the bathroom. Vanity sinks can be surface-mounted or under-mounted, which means the bowl is attached underneath the countertop. An integral sink combines the countertop material and the bowl (typically a solid-surface laminate) in one seamless piece. This makes for easy cleanup. With one sweep of the sponge, the countertop and sink are clean.

STORAGE You need to be creative about storage, especially if the bathroom will be small. Keeping the deck of the sink or the vanity top clear of clutter is important. Look for a medicine cabinet with extra-deep shelves that can accommodate rolls of toilet paper, as well as bulky blow dryers. Install wall shelves or use a three-tiered wire hanging basket to store cosmetics, soaps, or extra hand towels. Use baskets to contain grooming items, cleaning products, or extra linens. Or look behind the bathroom door for extra space. A cabinet can be built into the corner for storage needs.

OPPOSITE TOP If you like pedestal sinks, make sure there's space on the sink deck for resting grooming items.

OPPOSITE CENTER Improved finishes keep fixtures such as this high-polished brass set looking like new longer.

OPPOSITE BOTTOM Kids' bathrooms should be free of potentional hazards. Use slip-proof tiles and good lighting.

RIGHT Be sure to include as much storage as possible in the space. If you're short on space, install wall cabinets.

resource guide

The following list of manufacturers and associations is meant to be a general guide to additional industry and product-related sources. It is not intended as a listing of products and manufacturers represented by the photographs in this book.

Ann Sacks Tile & Stone, *a division of Kohler, manufactures ceramic, glass, and stone tile.*
8120 NE 33rd Dr.
Portland, OR 97211
Phone: 800-278-8453
www.annsacks.com

Baltic Leisure *manufactures steam showers and saunas.*
601 Lincoln St.
P. O. Box 530
Oxford, PA 19363
Phone: 800-441-7147
www.balticleisure.com

Bilco *manufactures window wells and basement doors.*
P. O. Box 1203
New Haven, CT 06505
Phone: 203-934-6363
www.bilco.com

Brewster Wallcovering Co. *manufactures wallpaper, fabrics, and borders in many patterns and styles.*
67 Pacella Park Dr.
Randolph, MA 02368
Phone: 781-963-4800
www.brewsterwallcovering.com

Bush Furniture *manufactures home and office furniture.*
2081 N. Webb Rd.
Wichita, KS 67206
Phone: 877-683-9393
www.bush-furniture-online.com

Central Fireplace *manufactures freestanding and zero-clearance fireplaces.*
20502 160th St.
Greenbush, MN 56726
Phone: 800-248-4681
www.centralfireplace.com

Ethan Allen *manufactures indoor and outdoor furniture.*
Ethan Allen Dr.
P. O. Box 1966
Danbury, CT 06813
Phone: 203-743-8000
www.ethanallen.com

Florida Tile *manufactures ceramic tile.*
P. O. Box 447
Lakeland, FL 33802
Phone: 800-242-9042
www.floridatile.com

Finnleo *manufactures saunas, steam baths, and accessories.*
575 E. Cokato St.
Cokato, MN 55321
Phone: 800-346-6536
www.finnleo.com

Fisher & Paykel, Inc., *manufactures kitchen appliances.*
27 Hubble
Irvine, CA 92618
Phone: 888-936-7872
www.fisherpaykel.com

General Electric *manufactures electronics and appliances.*
Phone: 800-626-2000
www.ge.com

Haier America *manufactures major appliances and electronics, such as refrigerators, freezers, and wine cellars.*
1356 Broadway
New York, NY 10018
Phone: 877-377-3639
www.haieramerica.com

Hooker Furniture *manufactures home furniture.*
P. O. Box 4708
Martinsville, VA 24115
Phone: 276-656-3335
www.hookerfurniture.com

Ikea *is a nationwide retailer of home furnishings and accessories.*
www.ikea.com

Iron-a-way *manufactures built-in ironing centers.*
220 W. Jackson
Morton, IL 61550-1588
Phone: 309-266-7232
www.ironaway.com

Jacuzzi Inc. *manufactures spas and shower systems.*
14801 Quorum Dr., Ste. 550
Dallas, TX 75254
Phone: 800-288-4002
www.jacuzzi.com

Jenn-Air, *a division of Maytag, manufactures kitchen appliances.*
Maytag Customer Service
240 Edwards St.
Cleveland, TN 37311
Phone: 800-688-1100
www.jennair.com

Kohler Co. *manufactures plumbing products.*
444 Highland Dr.
Kohler, WI 53044
Phone: 800-456-4537
www.kohlerco.com

Kraftmaid Cabinetry, Inc., *manufactures cabinetry.*
P. O. Box 1055
Middlefield, OH 44062
Phone: 440-632-5333
www.kraftmaid.com

La-Z-Boy, Inc., *manufactures furniture including home-theater seating.*
1284 N. Telegraph Rd.
Monroe, MI 48162-3390
Phone: 734-241-4414
www.lazyboy.com

Madawaska Doors, Inc., *manufactures wood doors.*
3280 Caroga Dr.
Mississaug, ON L4V 1L4
Phone: 905-673-0108
www.madawaska-doors.com

Maytag *manufactures major appliances.*
240 Edwards St.
Cleveland, TN 37311
Phone: 800-688-9900
www.maytag.com

Nautilus *manufactures exercise equipment such as the Stairmaster.*
1886 Prarie Wy.
Louisville, CO 80027
Phone: 800-688-9991
www.nautilus.com

Osram-Sylvania *manufactures lighting products and accessories.*
100 Endicott St.
Danvers, MA 01923
Phone: 978-777-1900
www.sylvania.com

Precor USA *manufactures cardiovascular fitness equipment, such as elliptical trainers, for residential and commercial use.*
P. O. Box 7202
Woodinville, WA 98072
Phone: 800-786-8404
www.precor.com

Resist-a-ball *manufactures fitness stability balls and offers exercise workshops and courses for consumers.*
4507 Furling Lane, Unit 201
Destin, FL 32541
Phone: 877-269-9893
www.resistaball.com

Rubbermaid *manufactures home-organizational products such as portable cabinets, storage bins, and toolboxes.*
1147 Akron Rd.
Wooster, OH 44691
Phone: 888-895-2110
www.rubbermaid.com

Sony *manufactures electronics such as TVs and DVD players.*
550 Madison Ave., 33rd Floor
New York, NY 10022
Phone: 800-222-7669
www.sony.com

Stanley Furniture *manufactures entertainment centers and other home furniture.*

1641 Fairystone Park Hwy.
Stanleytown, VA 24168
Phone: 276-627-2100
www.stanley.com

Steven Fuller, Inc., *is an architectural firm that specializes in residential architecture and design.*
4179 Pleasant Hill Rd.
Duluth, GA 30096
Phone: 800-274-2444
www.stephenfuller.com

Stickley Furniture *manufactures home furniture, rugs, and upholstery.*
1 Stickley Dr.
P. O. Box 480
Manlius, NY 13104-0480
Phone: 315-682-5500
www.stickley.com

Sure-Fit, Inc., *manufactures ready-made slipcovers and pillows.*
7339 Industrial Blvd.
Allentown, PA 18106
Phone: 888-754-7166
www.surefit.com

Therma-Tru Doors *manufactures exterior doors for residential use.*
1687 Woodlands Dr.
Maumee, OH 43537
Phone: 800-537-8827
www.thermatru.com

Thomasville Furniture Industries *manufactures wood and upholstered furniture and case goods.*
P. O. Box 339
Thomasville, NC 27361Phone: 800-225-0265
www.thomasville.com

WarmaTowel, *a division of Sussman, manufactures towel-warming metal racks.*
Nortesco, Inc.
151 Carlingview Dr., Unit 12
Rexdale, ON M9W 5S4
Phone: 800-667-8372
www.nortesco.com/sussman/towel/towel.html

Wilsonart International, Inc., *manufactures plastic laminate and solid-surfacing material.*
2400 Wilson Place
P. O. Box 6110
Temple, TX 76503
Phone: 800-433-3222
www.wilsonart.com

Whirlpool *manufactures major appliances, including washers and dryers.*
2000 N. M-63
Benton Harbor, MI 49022
Phone: 269-923-5000
www. whirlpool.com

index

glossary

Accent lighting Lighting that highlights a space or object to emphasize its character.

Armoire A solid cabinet, usually made of wood, that holds entertainment equipment or clothing.

Ambient light Also called general light, this overall light fills an entire room.

Awning window A single-sash window with a crank that swings outward and is hinged at the top.

Bifold door A hinged door, usually on a closet, that folds to the sides when opened.

Bulkhead door A sloping metal door that opens up from both sides and covers an exterior stairway into a basement.

Casement window A single-sash window that is vertically hinged and opens out.

Column A vertical support in a building frame, made of wood, metal, or concrete.

Drywall Gypsum sandwiched between treated paper, used as an interior wall covering. Also called gypsum board or wallboard.

Dehumidifier A machine that reduces the amount of moisture in the air.

Double-hung window A window with one or a pair of movable sash that slide vertically within the frame.

Drop ceiling A ceiling that is suspended and hides eyesores such as electrical wires.

Glass block Decorative building blocks made of translucent glass or acrylic for windows or non-load-bearing walls.

Ground-fault circuit interrupter (GFCI) A safety circuit breaker that compares the amount of current entering a receptacle with the amount leaving. If there is a discrepancy of 0.005 volt, the GFCI breaks the circuit in a fraction of a second. GFCIs are required by the National Electrical Code in areas that are subject to dampness.

French door A door, typically with 12 divided panes of glass. It can be used alone or in pairs or as a fixed window.

Glider A window with two sash that are set horizontally into a track to slide past each other within one frame. (Also called a slider.)

Hopper A window that is hinged at the bottom and tilts in when it is open. This is the most common type of basement window.

Impact-resistant glass Interlayers of laminated glass within an exceptionally strong frame that is designed to withstand shattering when stuck by a hard, forceful object or wind.

Laminated glass Two or three layers of glass with interlayers of plastic or resin, which hold fragments together if the glass shatters.

Louver door A framed door with horizontal slats for admitting air or light.

Murphy bed A bed that folds into the wall or a closet when not in use.

Opaque shade A lamp shade that only allows light to escape through the top and bottom.

Paper shade A lamp shade that allows an abundant amount of light through and often gives the room a soft glow.

Pendant Fixtures that hang down from the ceiling and direct light upward or downward.

Pocket door A door that slides into the wall when it is open.

Recessed light A light that has canister-style housing and is recessed into the ceiling.

Sconce A decorative wall light that usually focuses light toward the ceiling.

Single-hung window A window with two sash; the bottom one is operable and the top one is stationary.

Tambour door A cabinet door that is on a track and rolls up or down.

Task lighting Lighting that focuses on a specific area, such as a computer desk or a work table.

Torchère A tall floor lamp that resembles a torch and directs light toward the ceiling.

Translucent shade A lamp shade that diffuses light.

Trompe l'oeil French for "fools the eye." A style of painting that gives the viewer the illusion of reality.

Watt Unit of measurement of electrical power required or consumed by a fixture or appliance.

Window well A well, sometimes with levels or terraces, that leads to a basement window, allowing natural light to enter into the space.

Veneer A thin surface layer used on cabinetry and furniture.

photo & design credits

All photography by Phillip H. Ennis Photography, unless otherwise noted.

Cover: designer: Norman Michaeloff, ceiling by Andrew Tedesco **page 1:** courtesy of Osram-Sylvania, furniture by Ethan Allen **page 2:** designer: James Alan Smith **pages 6-7:** *left* designer: TK Theaters/Theo Kalomirakis; *center* designer: Libby Cameron; *right* courtesy of Osram-Sylvania **pages 8, 10, & 11:** designer: Anne Cooper Interiors **pages 12-13:** designer: Audio Design Assoc./Justin Baxter **page 14:** designer: Beverly Ellsley **page 15:** designer: Blodgett Designs **page 16:** designer: Rita Grants **page 17:** *top* designer: Siskin-Valls, Inc. **page 18:** designer: Richard Mishaan Designs **page 20:** *top* designer: Marie-Paule Pelle; *bottom* courtesy of Bilco **page 21:** *top* courtesy of Madawaska Doors; *bottom* courtesy of Whirlpool **pages 22-23:** *top left* designer: Kenneth Rendell Gallery; *bottom right* courtesy of Haier America; *center right* designer: Diane Boyer/Behrle Assoc.; *center left* designer: Boxwood & Ivy; *bottom left* designers: Design Consultants **page 24:** designer: Cynthia Bogart Wladyka **page 25:** *top* designer: Richard Mishaan; *bottom* designer: Green & Co./Gail Green **page 26:** *top* designer: James Alan Smith; *bottom* courtesy of Florida Tile **page 27:** *left* designer: Curb Gardner/Curb Gardner Collection; *right* designer: Stark Carpet/John Barman **page 28:** designer: Barbara Ostrom & Assoc. **page 29:** *top* Green & Co./Gail Green; *bottom* courtesy of Central Fireplace **page 30:** *left* architects: Andrew Chary & Assoc.; *right* courtesy of Ikea **page 31:** *top* designer: KJS Interiors; *bottom* courtesy of Ikea **page 32:** designer: Lexis Interiors; **page 34:** designer: TK Theaters, Inc./Theo Kalomirakis **pages 35, 36, & 37:** courtesy of Bilco **page 38:** designer: TK Theaters, Inc./Theo Kalomirakis **page 39:** designer: Ronald Bricke & Assoc. **page 40:** *right* courtesy of Therma-Tru Doors **page 41:** *top* designer: Robert DeCarlo **pages 44-45:** *top left* courtesy of Ikea; *top right* designer: Mike Nichols; *bottom* designer: Nicholas Calder **page 46:** designer: Don Schermehorn **page 47:** *top* designer: TK Theaters/Theo Kalomirakis; *bottom* architects: Dineen Nealy Architects **page 48:** *left* designer: Green & Co./Gail Green; *right* designer: Barbara Ostrom and Assoc.; *bottom* courtesy of Ikea **page 49:** designer: Audio Command Systems **page 50:** courtesy of Ikea **page 51:** *bottom* designer: Robert DeCarlo **page 52:** *top* designer: Stark Carpet/Kenneth Alpert; *bottom* designer: Samuel Botero & Assoc. **page 53:** *right* courtesy of Ikea; *bottom left*

designer: Tania Vartan **page 54:** *left* designer: Beverly Ellsley; *right* designer: Green & Co./Gail Green **page 55:** *left* designer: Lucretia Moroni, Ltd.; *top right* courtesy of GE; *bottom right* designer: Christopher Coleman **page 57:** *top* designer: Vogel/Mulea Designs; *bottom* courtesy of Osram-Sylvania **page 58:** courtesy of Osram-Sylvania **page 59:** designer: Robert DeCarlo **page 60:** courtesy of Kraftmaid Cabinetry, Inc. **pages 62-63:** *left* courtesy of La-Z-Boy; *center* courtesy of Kraftmaid Cabinetry, Inc.; *right* courtesy of Thomasville Furniture **page 64:** *top* courtesy Hooker Furniture; *bottom* courtesy of Ikea **page 65:** courtesy of Osram-Sylvania **page 66:** *top* courtesy of Stickley Furniture; *bottom* courtesy of Stanley Furniture **page 67:** *top* courtesy of Kraftmaid Cabinetry, Inc.; *bottom* courtesy of La-Z-Boy **page 68:** designer: Audio Command Systems **page 69:** *top* designer: TK Theaters, Inc./Theo Kalomirakis; *bottom* courtesy of Sure-Fit **page 70:** designer: TK Theaters, Inc./Theo Kalomirakis **page 72:** designer: Greenbaum Interiors/Lynn Cone, architects: Moisan Architects **page 73:** courtesy of Sony **page 74:** courtesy of Kraftmaid Cabinetry, Inc. **page 75:** *top* Audio Command Systems; *bottom* designer: TK Theaters, Inc./Theo Kalomirakis **page 76 & 78:** courtesy of Whirlpool **page 79:** *top* courtesy of Thomasville Furniture; *bottom* illustration courtesy of Whirlpool, illustration by Stephen Fuller, Inc. **pages 80-81:** *left* courtesy of Sure-Fit; *center* courtesy of Ikea; *right* courtesy of Thomasville Furniture **page 82:** courtesy of Stanley Furniture **page 83:** courtesy of Sure-Fit **page 84:** courtesy of GE **page 85:** courtesy of Maytag **pages 86-87:** *left* courtesy of Maytag; *top right* courtesy of Whirlpool; *bottom right* courtesy of Wilsonart International; *bottom center* courtesy of Osram-Sylvania **page 88:** *top* courtesy of Whirlpool; *bottom right* courtesy of Ironaway; *bottom left* designer: Reger Designs **page 89:** courtesy of Whirlpool **page 92:** designer: Susan Zises Green **page 93:** *top left* designer: Ken Hockin Interior Design; *top right* courtesy of Brewster Wallcoverings **page 95:** designer: Albert Pensis **page 96:** *top* designer: Cynthia, Inc. **page 97:** *top left* courtesy of Rubbermaid; *top right* architects: Mojo Stumer Architects; *bottom* courtesy of Osram-Sylvania **page 98:** courtesy of Osram-Sylvania, *top* furniture by Ethan Allen **page 99:** designer: Design 1/Merilee Schempp **page 100:** designer: Nicholas Calder & Assoc. **page 101:** *top* architect: Stuart Narofsky; *bottom* designer: Bernita Interiors, architect: Charles Rabinovitch **page**

102: courtesy of Kraftmaid Cabinetry, Inc. **page 104:** architects: Andrew Chary & Assoc. **page 105:** *top row* courtesy of Osram-Sylvania; *bottom* designer: Bernita Interiors **page 106:** designer: Design 1/Merilee Schempp **page 107:** *left* designer: Cooper Group; *right* designer: Richard Mishaan Designs **pages 108-109:** *center* courtesy of Ikea; *top and bottom right* courtesy of Rubbermaid **page 110:** courtesy of Haier America **page 111:** *top* courtesy of Rubbermaid; *bottom* courtesy of Osram-Sylvania **pages 112-113:** courtesy of Rubbermaid **page 114:** courtesy of Kohler Co. **page 116:** *top* designer: Vogel Mulea Designs; *bottom right* courtesy of Precor; *bottom left* designer: Siskin-Valls, Inc. **page 117:** courtesy of Nautilus **page 118:** *top* courtesy of Jacuzzi, Inc.; *bottom* courtesy of Ann Sacks Tile Co. **page 119:** courtesy of Ultra Bath **page 120:** *top* courtesy of Kohler Co.; *bottom* courtesy of Baltic Leisure **page 121:** courtesy of Kohler Co. **pages 122-123:** *top left* designer: Greenbaum Interiors/Lynn Cone; *top right* courtesy of Finnleo; *bottom* courtesy of Kohler Co. **page 124:** courtesy of WarmaTowel **page 125:** *left* courtesy of Baltic Leisure; *right* courtesy of Cielo **page 126:** designer: Green & Co./Gail Green **pages 128-129:** *top left* courtesy of Sharp; *top right and bottom* courtesy of Ikea **page 130:** *left* courtesy of Ikea; *top right and bottom right* courtesy of GE **page 131:** *top left* designer: Terrance Brennan; *center* manufacturer: Fisher & Paykel; *right* courtesy of Jenn-Air **page 132:** *left* designer: Green & Co./Gail Green; *right* designer: NDM Kitchens/Nancy Mullan **page 133:** *top* designer: Design Logic; *bottom* designer: Green & Co./Gail Green **page 134:** *top* courtesy of Kohler Co.; *bottom* designer: Reger Designs **page 135:** *top left* designer: Kemp-Simmons; *top right* designer: Richard Mervis; *bottom* designer: Blodgette Hatley **page 136:** *top* designer: Kat Interiors; *center and bottom* courtesy of Kohler Co. **page 137:** courtesy of Ikea

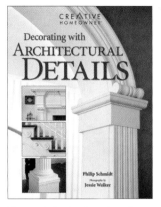
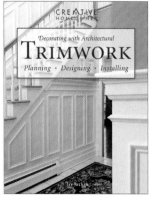
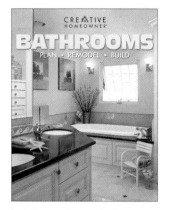

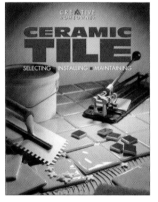

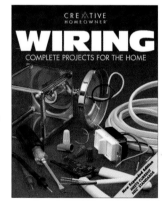
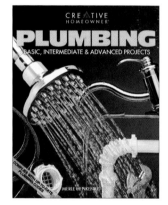
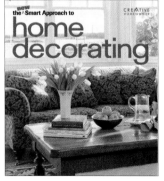